Building Parent Involvement
THROUGH THE ARTS

Building Parent Involvement
THROUGH THE ARTS

Activities and Projects That Enrich Classrooms and Schools

MICHAEL SIKES
FOREWORD BY RICHARD DEASY

CORWIN PRESS
A SAGE Publications Company
Thousand Oaks, CA 91320

For information:

Corwin Press
A Sage Publications Company
2455 Teller Road
Thousand Oaks, California 91320
www.corwinpress.com

Sage Publications Ltd.
1 Oliver's Yard
55 City Road
London EC1Y 1SP
United Kingdom

Sage Publications India Pvt. Ltd.
B–42, Panchsheel Enclave
Post Box 4109
New Delhi 110 017 India

Printed in the United States of America

Library of Congress Cataloging-in-Publication Data

Sikes, Michael.
Building parent involvement through the arts: Activities and projects that enrich classrooms and schools / Michael Sikes.
   p. cm.
Includes bibliographical references and index.
ISBN 1-4129-3682-9; 978-1-4129-3682-8 (cloth) — ISBN 1-4129-3683-7; 978-1-4129-3683-5 (pbk.)
   1. Arts—Study and teaching (Elementary)—United States. 2. Education, Elementary—Activity programs—United States. I. Title.
NX303.S55 2007
372.5—dc22

2006018749

This book is printed on acid-free paper.

06 07 08 09 10 10 9 8 7 6 5 4 3 2 1

Acquisitions Editor:	Rachel Livsey
Editorial Assistant:	Phyllis Cappello
Production Editor:	Melanie Birdsall
Typesetter:	C&M Digitals (P) Ltd.
Copy Editor:	Marilyn Power Scott
Proofreader:	Jenny Withers
Indexer:	Nara Wood
Cover Designer:	Lisa Miller

Contents

Foreword

The principal of an elementary school in Brooklyn, New York, told a group of researchers studying her school a favorite story that captures some of the advice Dr. Michael Sikes offers in this excellent book on how the arts can engage parents and families in the education of their children. Families at P.S. 130 speak 17 different languages. The school offers family art days to reach across the language and cultural differences that can make the school a daunting and intimidating place for many families. At one of the programs, an artist was teaching Chinese calligraphy. A student and her grandmother, both Chinese, attended the class. The grandmother, who did not speak English, saw that the artist was incorrectly rendering a Chinese character. The principal said the grandmother mustered her courage, walked to the front of the room, took the brush from the artist, and wrote the character correctly. It was a transformative moment, the principal said, not only for the grandmother, who "spoke" through her skill to all those in class, but for her granddaughter, who saw her teach, and to the school personnel who understood the potential for fully engaging her in school activities. The grandmother had never felt comfortable at the school before, blocked by her lack of English. "That experience made her part of the (school) community," the principal said; it gave her a way to contribute to its life and to the education of her granddaughter. "She was welcomed into the building," the principal added.

Schools know that they need the active involvement of parents and families if they are to succeed in reaching every child. The question is how to do it. It's not easy. The school must be a welcoming place that creates both a sense of belonging and contexts within which parents and families feel they are making a constructive—and appreciated—contribution. They need the delight of seeing their children succeed and the knowledge that they play active roles in making that happen in the school and at home.

Dr. Sikes in this book points to the solid body of research that demonstrates the power of the arts to create bonding experiences for schools, families, and students that lead to student achievement. And he draws lessons from his own personal and professional successes to provide specific and practical guidance to schools and parents on how to create and sustain those experiences and their impact. This is a much-needed book, and he is to be thanked for writing it.

—Richard Deasy
Director, Arts Education Partnership

Richard Deasy is the coauthor with Lauren M. Stevenson of Third Space: When Learning Matters, *a research study of how the arts transform schools by creating communities of learners among students, teachers, and parents.*

Preface

In 1993, the Arizona Commission on the Arts hired me to evaluate its Artist-in-Residence Program. For six months I traveled to different parts of the state, including urban Phoenix, rural Maricopa County, the pine-studded Coloradan Plateau, and the desert outskirts of Tucson. I collected extensive ethnographic data through observations and interviews. I found many fine examples of artists working with students to bring about extraordinary arts learning.

I found something else extraordinary: these programs were pulling parents and community members into the schools in ways they never had been before. Parents were volunteering; they were enthusiastic audience members; and they were collaborators with teachers and students in rich, arts-based projects. Time and again, my observations of these effects were confirmed by the testimony of teachers, administrators, artists, and the parents themselves. Later, in many other evaluations in the District of Columbia, Idaho, North Carolina, and Washington State, I saw these effects repeated.

Today we know that parent involvement is an indispensable ingredient in the menu of student success. The No Child Left Behind Act (NCLB; 2002) recognizes this and makes it a core requirement of federal funding. And yet the engagement and often even the presence of parents remain elusive in many schools and districts. What then is the potent magic that will make this happen?

I believe that the answer, or a large piece of it, has always been right in front of us. It is the development and maintenance of good arts programs. This approach has all of the attributes of a good solution: as I demonstrate in this book, it works—consistently and significantly. It is politically acceptable, as hardly anyone anywhere does not appreciate and value some form of artistic expression. It brings about important outcomes for students by helping them learn. And in contrast to the many costly interventions schools have tried and continue to try, beginning an arts program can be relatively inexpensive.

Building Parent Involvement Through the Arts is designed to help make such programs a reality. It is intended for school administrators, teachers, and parents. It may also be very relevant to community arts and cultural organizations that work in partnership with schools (including museums, libraries, and arts organizations). It is designed as a ready-to-use tool kit of simple steps. It is not primarily a research publication, exploring the *why*, which is documented amply elsewhere, although several of its chapters explore the research base.

Instead, it is mainly designed as an action-planning tool kit focusing on the *how*.

This book helps you to design and implement a program that uses the arts to increase family involvement. Chapter 1 summarizes what we know about the interconnections of the arts, parents, schools, and learning. Much of this current knowledge is reflected in federal and state programs, most notably NCLB, which mandates significant parent involvement outcomes as part of school reform.

Chapter 2 explores the many ways in which the arts create welcoming schools for parents and family members through the alteration of school cultures, and it looks at the exciting research emerging about the role of the arts in student achievement and the implications for parent involvement.

After these introductory chapters, the book moves more directly into applications. Chapters 3 through 7 describe ways to develop programs in visual art, theater, dance, music, and literary arts. Chapter 8 looks at folk and traditional arts from the same applied how-to perspective, with some additional explorations of the multicultural implications of traditional arts and their power to bond home to school. Each of these chapters includes specific project ideas and lesson plans.

From the traditional arts, Chapter 9 transitions to a consideration of ways to utilize community resources, including the wealth of arts organizations that many schools have at their doorsteps. Chapter 10 lays out specific plans for designing spaces for engaged learning and parent involvement, including arts-based classrooms and arts-based family centers. Chapter 10 also discusses the exciting potential of schools as centers of adult education in the arts.

Chapter 11 tells you how to begin planning, starting with an assessment of your school's current status and potential. It continues with specific guidance in developing integrated curricula and finding funding and support for your program. Chapter 12 explains how to evaluate your progress.

Throughout these chapters, *Building Parent Involvement* provides tools, templates, and forms for direct use in planning and creating programs. These complement the lesson plans and detailed project steps. It is hoped that through this design, practitioners will find this book not only readable but eminently practical on a daily basis.

Last, no work reflects a totally objective view of the world, unfiltered by the life experiences and critical judgments of its creator. Thus a word is in order about my philosophical stance and the approach of this book: in *Building Parent Involvement*, these precepts will be obvious and may provide comfort to some and discomfort to others. For example, purists, those who come from an *haute* culture view of the arts, may find occasional discomfort in this book's ready acceptance of pop culture and crafts as equally at home at the arts table. But my view is that the arts are as vital, organic, and ceaselessly changing as the peoples who gave life to them. After all, yesterday's bawdy entertainment in the Globe Theatre is today's Shakespearian masterpiece, and the barbaric thundering of an upstart nineteenth-century German pianist is today's Symphony No. 5 in C minor by Beethoven.

It is hoped that by reading a little more deeply, the guardians of high culture will find that behind the catholicity and openness of this book lies a deep reverence for the traditions and treasures that we have brought along on our human journey. Some are in the Louvre under glass, and some—maybe the next ones to be revered—are in the streets of our cities.

Acknowledgments

Any book that treats an area as vast and comprehensive as bridging schools and communities must represent the ideas of many contributors, collaborators, and creative voices. They include Mary Campbell-Zopf, Nancy Pistone, Ruth Piispanen, Sandie Campolo, and Linda Bellon-Fisher, all of whom have over the years afforded me rich opportunities to study the interactions of the arts and parental engagement in the programs under their stewardship. The many artists and educators with whom I have worked, especially over four years in Charlotte, North Carolina, provided me with deep insights about school and community linkages. The educators and children of the two Museum Magnet Schools in Washington, DC, showed me how to make a school an alive and welcoming place.

Rachel Livsey, Acquisitions Editor at Corwin Press, was perceptive of this book's promise, and her early encouragement and support were fundamental to its going forward. Several fine scholars lent a critical eye to various sections of the book concerning the various disciplines: Deb Brzoska in dance, Carol Myers in music, and Corwin Georges in theater. Ultimately, this project would not have been possible without my life partner Patti Frinzi, who recognized a book lurking inside a twenty-five-page outline and never stopped believing in it.

PUBLISHER'S ACKNOWLEDGMENTS

Corwin Press gratefully acknowledges the contributions of the following reviewers:

Donovan R. Walling
Director of Publications
Phi Delta Kappa International
Bloomington, IN

Marsha Greenfeld
Senior Instructional Facilitator
National Network of Partnership Schools at
    Johns Hopkins University
Baltimore, MD

Sally M. Wade
Director
Florida Partnership for Family Involvement in Education
University of South Florida
Tampa, FL

Wendy Caszatt-Allen
Eighth-Grade Language Arts Teacher
Mid-Prairie Middle School
Kalona, IA

Ilona Anderson
Principal
Flagstaff Middle School, An A+ School of Excellence
Flagstaff, AZ

James Kelleher
Assistant Superintendent
Scituate Public Schools
Scituate, MA

Diane W. Kyle
Professor
University of Louisville
Louisville, KY

Susan N. Imamura
Principal
Manoa Elementary School
Honolulu, HI

Mike Ford
Superintendent of Schools
Phelps-Clifton Springs Central School District
Clifton Springs, NY

About the Author

 **Michael Sikes** is an educational consultant primarily in the area of program evaluation, serves as adjunct faculty member at Antioch University Santa Barbara, and is former assistant director for education at the National Endowment for the Arts. For the past three years, he has been the principal evaluator for an international cultural exchange program of the Ohio Arts Council, sponsored by the U.S. Department of Education. Over the past decade, he has evaluated and researched cultural and arts programs across the United States and internationally. Coauthor of *The Appreciative Journey: A Guide to International Cultural Exchange*, Sikes received his doctoral degree in education from Florida State University.

Introduction

How the Arts Bring Parents Into Schools

The main office of a school is its public facade. It often reveals much of the school's inner workings, including its physical setting, the kinds of teaching and learning that take place, and the resources that are available to students. It may also be a key to the school's culture, a set of deeply embedded worldviews, beliefs, and values that guide the school and silently constrain all of its actions.

School cultures are not all the same. They vary across many dimensions. A pair of vignettes illustrates two particularly stark differences.

A VISIT TO TWO SCHOOLS

Maria has relocated to a new city and is visiting a couple of schools in order to select one for her daughter. Her first stop is at High Standards Elementary. She has heard that it has a good reputation for academics and fights to keep the test scores up. It is a disciplined, no-nonsense school that the principal runs with a laserlike focus on literacy and math.

When Maria arrives at the front office she has to wait behind a group of parents talking with the receptionist, who seems to be struggling to help the parents understand something about standards or assessments. Maria looks at the other office staff hopefully, but they all seem busy with administrative tasks. While she waits, she has time to make some observations.

The walls of the office are relatively sparse. No art, student work, or anything else indicates this place is about kids. Other than the discussion among the parents and the receptionist, there is little sound. Once, though, the intercom interrupts the quiet with an announcement that test results are due.

Finally Maria gets some attention. But the receptionist at first seems surprised that she would want to tour the school. After a few minutes she agrees to get someone to show her around.

Maria peers into a few of the classrooms. The kids are mostly doing seat work at their desks. The walls of the classrooms have relatively little student work on display. Occasionally she sees children walking from one room to another, evidently focused on their schoolwork, not smiling or talking. She is shown the library, the cafeteria, and the playground—which are largely empty of children except for those busy with assignments. Maria asks about art facilities, such as a music room. The guide replies that they have little time for such programs anymore. Moments later, Maria drives away, mentally striking this school off her list.

The next day, Maria goes out to Wide Horizons Academy, an alternative school a mile away from High Standards. Halfway through the office door, she receives the smiles of several people behind the desk. One of them summons the assistant principal, and introductions and welcomes quickly ensue. "Perhaps you'd like to tour our school . . . We usually start with the parent center," she's told.

For the next hour, Maria is amazed at what she sees. Everywhere, students are engaged in schoolwork that is clearly exciting and occasionally even noisy. The classrooms are splashed with color and art. Outside, there are gardens and natural areas where the teachers involve the students in science experiments. The sounds of children singing come from a music practice room.

The big surprise is that parents are everywhere. They assist as aides and tutors in the classrooms. She sees them in the art room, helping with a mural and serving as co-curators for an exhibition of student work being hung in the hall. They are in the cafeteria at lunchtime eating with the students. Some of them help students tend the garden or recycle. In the parent center, they help plan curricular activities and discuss assessment results. At length, the tour winds back to the office, where the assistant principal asks Maria, "So do you think you might want to send your daughter here?"

"Absolutely," Maria beams. "And I want to come, too."

THE WELCOMING SCHOOL

This story, though fictional, distils much of what is known about the public personae of schools. Almost everyone has probably gone into the first type of school and waited for acknowledgment. For some parents, moreover, such discomfort may bring back their own childhood memories of the school office as a place they would never want to have to go. All too often, what happens in the offices of today perpetuates this foreboding memory.

But a welcoming school is different. In such a school, the front office is a gathering place where visitors are greeted with eagerness rather than suspicion, find smiles rather than exasperated sighs, and see abundant student artwork and other evidence that children—and by inference, their parents—are valued there.

What explains the difference between these two types of schools? Both are in middle-class, suburban neighborhoods with no great disparities in funding. Both are in reasonably good buildings. But as we examine the differences, we find that the schools diverge most widely on two indisputable dimensions: *parent involvement* and *the arts.*

THE ROLE OF THE ARTS

In what ways are these two variables connected? Does the presence of the arts cause parents to become more involved in their children's schools? Does the active participation of parents lead to a greater presence of the arts? Or do both of these conditions stem from some third cause?

For me, the answer to these questions emerged on an evening a decade ago, when I observed an event at Brent Elementary, an inner-city Washington, DC, public school whose students were predominantly African American. This school was part of the Smithsonian Institution's Museum Magnet School Program, and this event was not the usual parents' night but the opening reception of a schoolwide museum exhibition built entirely by the hands and talents of students.

Entering the building, I had the immediate impression that this was no longer a school in the ordinary sense. Every classroom, every square foot of the halls, every space in the cafeteria was filled with objects. All of them were made by the students: pyramids, mummies, masks, images of Egyptian deities, Nile boats, flowers, papyrus, obelisks, objects for writing—visual testaments to the various things they had learned about the history and culture of ancient Egypt over three months of integrated study, jointly led by their own classroom teachers and Smithsonian curators and educators.

Already many parents had arrived. They moved eagerly from one room to the next, engaging the children, talking with them, complimenting them on their work. Teachers stood by their students and drank in the praise. Students were involved in every area of the school, conducting parents on tours, talking about objects, giving demonstrations, being curators themselves, participating in living history.

The extraordinary scene itself, the Egyptology displays, and the students seemed to melt into the background, and one thing stood out: the excitement— sensuous, palpable, and pulsing—of parents in the midst of a collective realization of the potential of their children for creativity, achievement, and success. For many, it was the first time.

From this scene the realization came to me: *the arts make student learning visible.* And the visibility attracts parents. Moreover, the effect seems remarkably consistent across regions, cultures, and peoples. The proud parents at the Smithsonian school were mostly African American. But Latino parents in California, Native American parents in Washington state, suburban parents in Idaho, and rural Mormon parents in Arizona all felt the same surge of pride in their children and the intensified connection with their children's schools when the arts came powerfully into play as the catalysts.

Research confirms that community-based arts and cultural resources and programs can enhance parent involvement. A number of mechanisms help make this happen. For example, arts programs often culminate in public performances or exhibitions to which parents are invited. Arts projects provide ways for communicating the achievement of standards and assessment results in ways that parents can understand. Large, interdisciplinary projects can involve entire communities. Folklore and local history can provide powerful ways for schools to connect with family and community members. Cultural organizations frequently have deep community connections—especially those that represent specific cultural groups with long traditions, such as a local Hispanic or African American cultural center. And the list goes on.

HOW THE ARTS CREATE WELCOMING SCHOOLS

So a strong relationship connects the arts and parent involvement. Ironically, most of the official programs that seek to involve parents approach the problem from the standpoint that parents understand schooling and want to be there except for obstacles in their own lives, such as conflicts with work. This book takes a different approach, based on the belief that schools can be inherently welcoming or unwelcoming, depending on how they approach the following conditions:

1. Standards-based education, dry and stultified by the bureaucratic language in which it is framed, can be mystifying to laypersons.

2. Parents often find schools unfriendly and unwelcoming.

3. Some parents, especially in traditional minority cultures, perceive schools as off-limits, where expert teachers are beyond question.

4. Minority cultures see themselves as marginalized and less central to the school's work.

Here are some ways that the arts can help rectify these conditions:

1. Standards-based education can come alive when expressed in accessible language and illuminated via student work, including writing, visual art projects, and performances.

2. Schools can create atmospheres that are friendly and enjoyable, where student work is continuously celebrated.

3. Parents can be invited to see schools as places where they have a role in initiating ideas and planning.

4. All cultures can be valued as important in the school.

In short, parent involvement and the arts and culture are linked. The arts can even invite parents to become involved with other subject areas. So it is beyond merely important—rather, it is essential—that schools learn to tap this important power.

THE MANY ROLES OF PARENTS

As a prerequisite to integrating families into the vital daily life of schools, it is important to fully understand how parents impact their children's learning when they are fully engaged and how they often fail to have much effect when they are not.

If parents or family members are actively engaged in and committed to their children's schools, the schools are better places and the students perform better academically. Ample evidence supports this point. When parents come to school and demonstrate interest in what their children are doing, they signal to the students that the hours they spend in school and the work that occupies their time there are important and to be valued. Moreover, this interaction has a reciprocal effect on parents. By gaining a clearer idea of what schools and teachers are trying to do, they become better partners in the educational enterprise and provide better support at home. Last, parents as volunteers provide invaluable extra resources—both in time and energy—that would not otherwise be available to hard-pressed schools.

PARENTS AND BETTER SCHOOLS

Research has established a strong correlation between parent engagement and school quality. The U.S. Department of Education and the North Central Regional Educational Laboratory provide annotated bibliographies and sources on the connection between parents and several indicators of school effectiveness; both are available via the Web. Briefly, some of these effects may be summarized as follows:

- Student achievement and students' attitudes toward school and learning improve.
- Student attendance increases, along with a concomitant reduction in discipline problems.
- Students appear to develop higher aspirations for their schoolwork.
- Parents develop deeper understandings of what their children are being taught.
- Parents express a greater obligation to help their children with homework.
- Parents are more positive about the interpersonal skills of their students' teachers.
- Parents rate their students' teachers higher in overall teaching ability and their schools higher in overall quality.
- These effects take place irrespective of socioeconomic status. (North Central Educational Laboratory, 2006)

Narrowing our focus a little, we can see from the research that parents play an enormous role in their children's success in school. For example, Bransford, Brown, and Cocking (2000) note the following:

> Learner-centered environments attempt to help students make connections between their previous knowledge and their current academic tasks. Parents are especially good at helping their children make connections. Teachers have a harder time because they do not share the life experiences of each of their students. (p. 153)

GETTING TO KNOW PARENTS

Many channels, formal and informal, exist for learning more about parents. NCLB and the various state and district plans that it has fostered require parent participation in school governance. School site councils and parent-teacher organizations are other formal channels. So a clear mandate exists for schools in this area.

Extensive research has revealed six broad dimensions of parent involvement, which Epstein and her colleagues (2002) summarized in the following framework:

Type 1: Parenting. Helping parents to provide supportive home environments

Type 2: Communicating. Ensuring adequate communication between home and school

Type 3: Volunteering. Recruiting parents to help and support in the school

Type 4: Learning at Home. Supporting the role of parents as helpers in students' homework and projects

Type 5: Decision Making. Including parents in the school's decision-making processes

Type 6: Collaborating With the Community. Integrating community resources to support learning

The arts, however, go beyond this typology in two vital ways. They help fuse the often disparate cultures of the school and its communities and the families that live in them, and they can provide active roles for family members as tradition bearers and community-based educators in a wide variety of projects and lessons. This latter role reflects Type 6 but transcends it by assigning a place of honor to families for what they understand, know, and can do.

It is *not* a position of *Building Parent Involvement* that parents should take on the role of the classroom teacher. The well-recognized expectation that certificated teachers have the legal and rightful role of educating children finds ample support here. However, a prominent role remains for parents as guest artists or demonstrators of traditional knowledge, as in Chapter 8. In such circumstances the teacher lets go for a time and allows someone else the central role in the classroom, perhaps becoming a learner along with her students. This should not compromise a teacher's adherence to the legal mandate to meet standards. Effective instruction, especially at the highest levels, involves more than the delivery of content. It includes the skillful interweaving of various resources and sources of expertise—the teacher's own and that of others—into a thoughtful, engaging lesson.

Each of the above types or dimensions presents different challenges and opportunities (Epstein et al., 2002). In *Building Parent Involvement*, you can discover a variety of ways to engage parents that encompass each of these types. Perhaps one of the best ways is to learn more about your students' parents. Who are they? What do they do? What do they know and understand? What traditions, ideas, and cultural artifacts do they value? Chapters 3 through 8 help to answer such questions by weaving active parent roles into projects and lessons while offering extensive opportunities for volunteering and learning at home. Moreover, Chapter 8 includes several lessons that can provide firsthand experience with the many traditional arts that are practiced by people on a daily basis. Many of the chapters, especially Chapters 10 and 11, provide ways of involving parents in planning arts-based programs and spaces.

But before all this, it is important to understand that the arts have intrinsic value to schools, both to the learning that takes place there and the spaces in which it takes place. Chapter 2 briefly reviews what we know about these important connections.

2

The Arts, Parent Involvement, and Student Achievement

A Winning Equation

Having established that parents are critical to school and student success, let us consider the role of the arts in this equation. In fact, this role is multifaceted and multidimensional, as later chapters reveal. For now, it may be useful to consider these roles as constituting a long continuum of connections, one which starts outside of the entrance to the school and extends into the heart of the classroom. Here are some of the continuum's components:

- *Outside the School.* Public art, such as murals, sculpture, and installations, can invite visitors and even passersby to stop, look at works, and contemplate their meaning. This stimulates their curiosity and imagination.

- *In the School Office.* Prominent displays of student work communicate the values, aspirations, and visions of students and signify that the school's business center has a soul. And since the artwork of students is at least partially about parents as well, it shows that they are welcome and valued.

Photo 2.1 Entrance to Caldwell (Idaho) High School.
Photo by Jeanne Leffingwell.

- *In the Halls.* Displays of student work, either in cases or on walls, provide ongoing evidence of student artistry and documentation of extended units or lessons, festivals, celebrations, or performing arts events.

- *Into the Classrooms.* Artwork can provide coherent themes connecting the inside with the outside. Doors of rooms can be decorated with signage indicating that there is more to see inside, especially during open houses and parent nights. Inside the rooms, student work can be posted on walls and connected to assignments, projects, and content standards, along with rubrics and other assessment tools clarifying how the work demonstrates student mastery and achievement.

- *Performances.* In a gym, cafeteria, auditorium, multipurpose room, or dedicated space, such as a gallery (see Chapter 3) or a theater (see Chapter 4), student performing arts can engage parents as audience members. Performances that are open to the public can include dress rehearsals, recitals, weekend matinees, or opening night. An abundance of advance publicity, take-home flyers, press coverage, a theaterlike box office, ushers, and other real-world components can ensure greater attendance and a more realistic setting. Similarly, the opening of a student exhibition in the school's gallery can feature refreshments, an opening talk, and docent-led tours.

- *Volunteer Efforts.* Parents might serve as ushers, chaperones for a visit to a museum or arts center, teachers' aids in a lesson, and so on. In these roles, parents can learn alongside their children and gain confidence in working in the arts. Parents can provide essential skills in helping build dedicated performance and exhibition spaces.

- *Cooperative Learning.* Parents can work with their children in a variety of projects that not only invite but depend upon the extra hands and thoughts that a parent can bring to the task. Moreover, much of the real work in a unit or lesson goes home with the students in the form of homework assignments. Through the arts, parents can become involved, engaged mentors and colearners.

- *Folk Arts, Folklife, and Family History.* Each family and community is connected by powerful threads to its own history and culture. These connections can be explored through many different kinds of projects, including family folklife research, visiting demonstrations by parents, and community festivals. It is this latter pathway for parent involvement that is critically important in a time of great cultural pluralism and ethnic transformation. It is a topic that Chapter 8 explores in detail.

This continuum provides one way of thinking about the impact of the arts on schools. If the arts could provide us with pathways to bridge the school-community divide, powerfully engage parents, and bring about rich explorations of diversity—and this were all that they could do—they would be valuable agents for positive school change. However, a considerable and growing body of research indicates that they are good for much more, that in fact they significantly impact learning by enhancing student engagement and thinking. These connections are important, not just for their own sake but because they provide an additional level of incentive for parent engagement. While many of the contributions that the arts make to learning have been common knowledge for decades, others have only recently emerged from research. They provide an incredibly important value-added component that schools need to communicate to parents. The next section explores these connections in detail.

THE ARTS AND COGNITION

In the early 1990s, researchers at the University of California in Irvine (Rauscher, Shaw, & Ky, 1993) noticed an interesting phenomenon. As they studied the cognitive effects of music, they began uncovering a correlation between early music instruction and spatial reasoning. These findings, which seemed to have enormous potential for instruction in mathematics and science, triggered a minor revolution in popular conceptions of arts learning, the so-called Mozart effect.

This research was not without its detractors, many of whom were unable to replicate its findings under controlled conditions. And the jury is still out, although promising follow-up studies by Rauscher and Shaw (as cited in Deasy, 2002) seem to substantiate many of the early findings. Thus far, the most lasting consequence of this study and the publicity surrounding it is that they helped usher in a surge of interest in including the arts as suitable subjects for research. Extensive summaries (Deasy, 2002; Fiske, n.d.; Winner & Hetland, 2000) chronicle the extent and diversity of this research activity.

The body of research on the various roles the arts play in thinking and learning has expanded significantly in the past decade. Yet this research tradition goes back at least to Howard Gardner (1983/1993) who revolutionized educational psychology with his theory of multiple intelligences (MI). This theory claims that what we call *intelligence* actually consists of multiple strands—many of which correlate closely to arts forms—such as spatial, musical, bodily-kinesthetic, interpersonal, and intrapersonal. Some of these connections, such as musical intelligence and music education, are obvious. More subtle connections link interpersonal intelligence with theater and intrapersonal intelligence with all arts forms.

Gardner's (1983) theory had enormous influence on teaching and assessment in schools, both in the United States and abroad, with entire schools and their curricula designed around MI. Although criticized by some educators, MI has helped spark an expanded view of intelligence that encompasses higher-order thinking and thinking dispositions (Perkins & Tishman, 2001), emotional intelligence (Goleman, 1995), and neuropsychology (Jensen, 2001). All of these areas of study have implications for the arts.

Since the mid-1990s various scholars have conducted extensive research into the importance of the arts on learning in other subjects. This research includes contributions by Burton, Horowitz, and Abeles (2000); Catterall (2002); and Winner and Hetland (2000). Generally, these studies have supported at least some bases for concluding that the arts enhance learning in other areas. For example, Deasy (2002) demonstrates the arts' connections to a variety of cognitive skills that include teamwork and social learning, critical and higher-order thinking, and creativity. Credible evidence from this research suggests that if schools include standards-based arts instruction guided by appropriate scope and sequence, many students will realize significant benefits in these domains, which impact on student success in school and beyond.

Countering these claims somewhat, Elliot Eisner (2002) contends that the rightful contributions of the arts to learning are more intrinsic to the arts disciplines themselves. He cites six major effects that the arts bring to general intellectual development:

- Experiencing qualitative relationships and making judgments
- Being flexible in purpose
- Understanding interrelationships of form and content
- Understanding that not everything knowable can be articulated in propositional form
- Being open to constraints of the medium being used
- Appreciating aesthetic satisfactions the work itself makes possible (Eisner, 2002)

Why are these findings relevant to parent involvement? It is very simply this: articulated in ways that parents and laypersons can understand, they help shift the debate away from test scores while arming advocates—including engaged parents—with new understandings for conveying the value of public schools.

Why do cultural and arts lessons stimulate parts of the brain responsible for higher-level thinking? Although the connection is not totally clear, mounting evidence supports the theory that experiences in visual, performing, and literary arts as well as projects that connect students to their own cultures and heritage tap such constructs as empathy, perspective, self-knowledge, and the ability to see the big picture.

Consider the following math examples from state standards and how concrete experiences in the arts can make the abstract language come alive:

State Standards	Understandings Through the Arts
1.0 Students compute and analyze statistical measurements for data sets: 1.1 Compute the range, mean, median, and mode of data sets. 1.2 Understand how additional data added to data sets may affect these computations of measures of central tendency.	A collection of information or data is seldom random; rather, it has patterns that can be understood mathematically and visually. (Visual art)
2.0 Students use data samples of a population and describe the characteristics and limitations of the samples: 2.1 Compare different samples of a population with the data from the entire population and identify a situation in which it makes sense to use a sample.	Important decisions in life—for example, in public policy, marketing of goods, or the development of entertainment—are often based on the opinions of a few people who represent the society as a whole in that area. (Theater, creative writing)

The following is a summary, excerpted from recent reviews of the literature (Sikes, 2005b):

- The arts improve thinking skills of students, especially critical thinking. Students' arts experiences can help them develop evaluation and judgment, conceptualize and test theories, and examine hypotheses.
- Learning in drama and theater can enhance students' personal and social development and help them successfully transition to adulthood and fulfill their potential. It can develop risk taking, provide an opportunity to explore and express thoughts and feelings, and offer fuller participation in their communities.
- The arts can help students to develop and examine their own epistemologies—their theories of what they know and how they know it.

- Students can learn to discuss and understand cultural differences and similarities that impact how they see and interpret aesthetically.
- Learning in the arts can help students to form and understand multiple perspectives and complex, subtle relationships.
- The bringing together of multiple artistic traditions can develop more sophisticated thinking about other people and combat racism.
- The arts develop creative thinking, including divergent thinking, risk taking, discovery and pursuit of the right medium, and stylistic distinctiveness.

As research moves forward, we may soon see the day when the arts are the focus of lessons whose primary purpose is to foster thinking skills. And you do not need to wait for that day to come. The arts are tools waiting for your use.

Although their testing is not required under federal and state accountability provisions, the arts have significant potential for exciting student engagement with learning. Moreover, many students evidence an early interest in the arts and plan to have careers in artistic or creative disciplines. To meet the needs of these students, the content standards in the performing and visual arts (as well as the creative writing emphases in English language arts standards) are excellent guides for curricula and teaching and provide useful benchmarks for assessment. Information on the standards of any state is available through the Web site of the state Department of Education.

THE ARTS AND STANDARDS

Summing up what we've covered so far, the arts offer the following powerful benefits to schools:

1. They can cause parents to become engaged with schools and involved as partners with their children and their children's teachers.

2. They can connect children to their own cultures and the cultures of others.

3. They help students develop creativity, adaptability, and other ways of thinking and working that are correlates of future school and life success.

4. According to mounting evidence, the arts are linked to students' general academic success and specific achievement in other subject areas.

Given these advantages, it is not surprising that school board members, teachers, and administrators want to tap these powers in the daily life of their schools. But *want* is the operative word. While the desire is there, in the current climate of standards-based accountability propelled by NCLB, many find it difficult to teach anything that is not assessed in the high-stakes tests. For the present, that means only English language arts and math. (Science comes into the testing and test preparation loop in 2007.)

The arts, fortunately, have an escape clause: teachers can meet standards in many subjects through arts-infused lessons. In fact, the arts readily intersect with standards in English language arts, science, history/social studies, and math. Integrated lessons that blend the concepts of more than one subject reflect how people naturally think, engage student interest, and tap higher order thinking.

The arts are natural partners with other subjects. They intersect with other domains of knowledge because they can simultaneously function as realms of content in which laws and rules govern relationships (like math), systems of signification (like language), and modes of research (like science or history). Although many persons resist curricula integration—including persons in the arts who want to preserve a disciplinary purity or boundaries—the arts themselves seem perfectly comfortable in all of these roles and in the company of many disciplines, including the following:

- *Language Arts.* Visual art projects can powerfully interlock with language arts. The following standard would connect with most visual art lessons, whether they involve creating an original work, responding to existing art, or both: Uses viewing skills and strategies to understand and interpret visual media. (National Standards in English Language Arts; Kendall & Marzano, 2004). Moreover, the natural intersection of drama and English language arts makes them powerful partners.

- *Science.* The large-group lessons in Chapter 3 (about visual art) can be connected to local natural areas or environmental conditions or issues, thus meeting various science standards. For example, a mural could explore an ecology theme. Students would need to conduct preliminary research, thus meeting the following:

Students know that an organism's patterns of behavior are related to the nature of that organism's environment. Students know that good scientific explanations are based on evidence (observations) and scientific knowledge. (National Standards in Science; Kendall & Marzano, 2004)

- *History/Social Studies.* U.S., state, and local history can be the subjects of rich exploration via visual media. A mural, for example, can examine a historical event important to students and the community: Understands the contributions and significance of historical figures of the community (National Standards in History; Kendall & Marzano, 2004).

- *Math.* Arts projects can seamlessly integrate with both the concepts and tools of math. For example, students need to use measurement in many types of visual work: Selects and uses appropriate tools for given measurement situations (e.g., rulers for length, measuring cups for capacity, protractors for angle; National Standards in Mathematics; Kendall & Marzano, 2004).

Conceived and implemented with appropriate depth and complexity, such integrated teaching takes away nothing from either domain but in fact increases understanding of each. As an example that quickly reveals the subtle interconnections possible when you integrate subjects, consider Project Idea 2.1, a lesson that was developed in a Goleta, California, elementary math class.

Project Idea 2.1 | Designing a House

Subjects

Mathematics

Visual arts

Grade Level

5–6

Purpose or Rationale

Using a real-world project, students can learn to use math skills that help solve everyday problems.

Content Standards Addressed

- Measurement, including the use of measuring tools and the conversion between metric and English scales
- Geometry, including the calculation and plotting of angles
- Visual art, including two-dimensional and three-dimensional representation and selection of appropriate materials

Objectives

Students will apply mathematical operations of measurement, conversions between English and metric units, and graphing. Students will complete an original design for a house that reflects their own culture.

Materials

- Mat board
- Tape
- Rulers
- Graph paper

Grouping or Classroom Modification

Students work in teams of three to five at tables.

Parent or Family Role

In the design phase of this project, family members can help the children conduct the measurements of their own home.

Procedure

Show examples of domestic architecture from many cultures. Have a large-group discussion. What are the distinctive aspects of the different buildings?

As homework, have the students select a room in their houses and study it. In what ways is it like the buildings they discussed in class? Have them make careful measurements of the floor and all the walls. They should measure in feet and inches and write all of the dimensions down. They may want to make a diagram for accuracy.

Distribute mat board and tape to each team of students. Their assignment is to design a scale model of a room. They have to convert feet to centimeters. Then they draw each of the sides in small scale, using the centimeter measurements. After that, they need to scale each dimension up to a larger size, such as five times as big, and convert their measurements from centimeters to inches in the process. They have to accurately measure and cut out each side, including the floor and a roof, then tape them in. Each team keeps a record of their measurements and their intermediate diagrams and can explain every step of the way.

Have a group discussion: What dimensions do the various scale models and their surfaces include? What aesthetic qualities do these dimensions have?

Assessment

Students can be assessed on their participation and collaboration in group work, the accuracy of their mathematical computations and operations, and the quality of their designs.

Now having looked at a good example of integration, it is necessary to acknowledge the possibility of examples that are less fortunate—one that often occurs, unfortunately. I call the simplified bad example "The Dance of the Quadratic Equations." In such a lesson, students compute and graph a quadratic equation. They use various conceptual operations in mathematics and meet several of the standards in this discipline. Finally, "the arts" are brought in as a disconnected afterthought, as the students are asked to lie on the floor to demonstrate the shape of their graphs through the positions of their bodies!

You understand the difference: "Designing a House" is complex, exploring the conceptual interconnections among two realms of knowledge, geometry and architecture—an intersection of their essences, not just of their semblances. "Quadratic Equations" is a rough pastiche that poorly serves the math and badly misuses the art of movement.

So integrating at a high level is both a critical and an intensely creative act. It involves a rich engagement with two disciplines (or more than two, in some cases) and a thorough understanding of the meaning of the standards from which you must draw.

Some Criteria for Integration

Here are some criteria which you can use to gauge your own integrated lessons:

- The lesson meets standards in the multiple disciplines.
- The lesson teaches knowledge or skills that are at the heart of the disciplines.
- The various disciplines can be assessed using authentic measures.

The Arts and Basal Readers

"This is all fine," you may say. "But I've got a two-and-a-half-hour block of Houghton-Mifflin (or *Open Court*, or some other basal reader), and I have to follow their pacing guide." The writers and editors of *Open Court*, *Houghton-Mifflin Reading*, and other similar textbook series probably never intended to exclude the arts. (We can at least give them the benefit of the doubt.) However, they have generally had this effect. This is partly because of the widespread belief that nothing can be brought into the classroom to complement these readers, that anything from outside will take away valuable time needed for literacy. Whether this perception emanates from the teachers, the administrators, or the companies that train teachers to use the readers, in fact nothing could be further from the truth. The arts can actually strengthen the basal readers, as seen in Project Idea 2.2.

Drill and kill? Who needs it? You can teach better, students will understand more deeply, and their test-taking prowess should, if anything, increase through integrated curricula. So it is very important to understand that these projects are not fluff or entertainment but rather engaged learning. In countless examples across the country, arts educators have demonstrated the power of the arts to hook learners through alternative modalities and project-based learning.

Project Idea 2.2 Integrating Reading

Subjects

English language arts
Visual art
Theater

Grade Level

Multiple

Purpose or Rationale

Stories and books can be tremendously potent learning tools for students, helping them to see the world through someone else's eyes. The world of children's literature has been shown to have widespread appeal to students, especially if they have the opportunity to select their own reading.

In California, as in many states, students can't always select what they read because of state- and district-adopted reading series or basal readers. Many of these are filled with excellent reading, along with many good tools to help children deepen their reading experience. However, many stories, including those in state-adopted readers, are initially foreign to students, who have difficulty relating to or accepting the characters, settings, and situations that they find therein.

As the illustration to follow demonstrates, student resistance stemming from these cultural differences and the lack of perspective acts as a barrier to entry into the story, which could otherwise provide rich new understandings. Often the greater these potential understandings, the stronger the initial barrier. This is because perspective is such a strong and essential critical thinking skill. Thus its cultivation is vital to effective reading of literature.

An example is *Skylark* by Patricia MacLachlan (1994; a portion of which is included in the Houghton-Mifflin California Grade 4 reader). Although children are in many ways the same all over the world, this story is about a time and place that seems foreign to many of today's young people: the main characters live on a farm miles from the nearest neighbors in a world without cell phones or the Internet, their biggest concern being having enough water to grow crops.

To counter this strangeness, teachers can use a variety of perspective-building tools that help students to more easily enter an unfamiliar world.

Content Standards Addressed

- English language arts, including critical discussions of texts
- Visual arts, including drawing imaginary scenes based on a theme or idea
- Theater, including playwriting, group work, and acting

Objectives

- Students understand that people in stories and books are similar to themselves, even though they live in different times or places, and that they face the same kinds of challenges in their lives.
- Identify ways that characters in stories and books are similar to themselves.
- Describe ways that they relate to characters in their readings.

Materials

- Drawing materials

Grouping or Classroom Modification

Students work as a whole class and in small groups.

Parent or Family Role

Parents can participate actively with their children in recalling and thinking about the significance of a major family decision that can be relevant to understanding the lesson.

Procedure

After reading the selection, have the students work individually to draw their own pictures of life on the prairie during the time of *Skylark*. They should include themselves in the picture, depicting themselves in some active role. After completing the drawings, you may have each student present and talk about his or her work.

List some unfamiliar words from the story for students to look up: *phonograph* (we may remember phonograph records, but do children?) How did their music differ from ours?

Give the students the following prompt: "Recall a time in your own life when your family had to make a big decision, like moving to a new home or an entirely new town." As a homework assignment, the students can discuss this question with their parents or family members and write down a series of events related to the decision.

In small groups, have the students select one of the decisions and write a three-minute play. Have students take on characters in the play. Each team can then have the opportunity to read its play to the rest of the class.

Assessment

Students may be assessed on the quality and visual sophistication of their drawings, their group work, and their final performances.

An essential tool for developing lessons or units that integrate content areas at a high conceptual level is some form of lesson-planning template. *Building Parent Involvement* offers its own version, the Integrated Curriculum Planning Guide (see Chapter 11). It offers a way to build family involvement partnerships; meet complex, challenging state standards; and engage students—three essential goals in any school. This tool includes directions for its use and is followed immediately by a blank template version that you may use.

COMMUNICATING STANDARDS

One of the greatest challenges in the current wave of standards-based accountability is helping parents to understand what standards mean. The arts can be part of a comprehensive strategy for communicating standards to parents. Here are seven components of such a strategy:

1. Translate the Standards

Standards are important documents for parents. They should be able to understand them without having a degree in education. In the following example, two standards are conveyed in parent-friendly language:

National Standard: English Language Arts	Parent-Friendly Language
Students write compositions about autobiographical incidents, exploring the significance and personal importance of the incident and using details to provide a context for the incident.	Children use writing to describe and explain objects, events, and people from their own lives.
National Standard: Math	Parent-Friendly Language
Understand measures of central tendency.	Calculate the average of a group of numbers.

If students met the expectations in the right-hand column, they would also meet the standards in the left, while short-circuiting some of the educational jargon.

The other critical need, of course, is translation from English into other languages spoken at home, where necessary.

2. Provide Useful Metaphors of Standards From the Arts, Folklore, Their Culture, or Everyday Life

Parents ought to know that standards don't have to be mysterious. They are like many things common in everyday life. For example, when you do a handicraft project, when you cook a meal, or when you paint a wall of your house, you have a finished product in mind. People in business use standards when they establish mission statements and goals. Standards describe acceptable outcomes of a project or task. In education, standards describe the acceptable outcomes of children's education.

3. Provide Increased Opportunities for Parent Interaction

Parents need longer, deeper, and richer engagement with their children's learning and with the standards by which their work is measured. Many of the projects and lessons in this book seek to engage parents in standards-based work. Other events, such as Back-to-School Night, Literacy Night, or Family Art Day, provide additional opportunities for reinforcement. Post standards at exhibitions and performances and publish them in student literary journals. Provide posters and displays in various classrooms listing the standards, some translations of them—both into Spanish and into layperson's language—and examples of student work that meet the standards, including student artwork.

4. Answer the "Why"

Most people believe that standards are for educators. They provide guidance in what to teach and when. But parents need to understand that the standards are also for them. They provide parents with useful information on what their child is learning. A key question for parents is, *How are standards important for your child's future?* A good answer is, Standards provide everyone—students, parents, and teachers—with a common set of expectations to work toward.

5. Use Questions and Answers

You can prepare a list of frequently asked questions for parents, along with the answers. A brief set of such questions might include the following:

Q: What do standards mean for my child?

Q: How are standards tested?

Q: How can I prepare my child to meet standards and do better on tests?

In addition, through active questioning and engagement, parents can take ownership of standards-based education. They might ask their children's teachers the following:

- What do you do to help my child master the standards?
- What should my child be doing?
- What should I be doing to help?

6. Use Technology and Graphic-Rich Media

The power of the Internet as a medium of communication is indisputable. The Web can reach into almost any household that a school serves. Innovative teachers and administrators can craft Web sites that make standards come alive, providing explanations of standards and examples from student work. Moreover, the Web is not simply a static medium: it can communicate video and digital sound files of students' performances. Students, who are often as tech-savvy as teachers, can be eager partners in such creative communication. Many parents have technology training and can be brought into the process.

7. Provide a Place for Parents

Each school should have a place where parents can go. It can be a parent room, a kind of library of standards and student work for parents. While availability of space is always a problem, this might prove a welcoming entrée to parents visiting the campus. From there, they might visit classrooms to see examples in action. As outlined in Chapter 10, an arts-based family center can even provide a focal point for parental volunteerism and activism.

MOVING ON TO ARTS LESSONS

This chapter has given you a grounding in the general ways that the arts intersect with schools and the learning that goes on in them. The arts can transform school cultures and engage parents, boost student achievement, and foster higher-order thinking skills. This book has also begun to explain how integrated, thematic lessons can galvanize members of the school and even the community. The following chapters delve into the specifics of using visual art, theater, dance, music, and folk and traditional arts to bring about some of these outcomes.

3

Developing a Visual Arts Program

Since the Renaissance, educators have recognized that the visual arts are essential pathways to cognition. For young children, drawing provides a tool for description and expression before the development of literacy. In later years, the development of knowledge and skills in idea formation, expression, art criticism, and cultural awareness goes along with other essential strands of academic achievement.

VISUAL ARTS AND PARENT INVOLVEMENT

For parents, visual art projects provide tangible evidence of their children's achievements. From the earliest children's drawings displayed on the refrigerator door to complex visual works that explore their own lives, students' artwork provides an irreplaceable mode of communication to parents of achievement, skill, values, and hard work.

Regardless of the age and grade level and irrespective of the project type, the visual arts may offer numerous points of connection and welcome for parents, who might assist the regular classroom teacher in multiple stages of a lesson or work with students as a partner and team member. Parents may participate in planning an art project, take part in discussions and peer critiques, and even work alongside students in group projects. They can have roles as diverse as mentor, critic, curator, docent, and audience. Their work can be especially valuable in large projects like murals. While extensive expertise in visual art may be a welcomed attribute, it is never essential that parents have art backgrounds. Often they can learn along with the students.

It is also worth noting that, of the great variety of visual art projects possible in a classroom, many do not require an art specialist or visiting artist. In many cases, K–8 teachers may find that they can readily craft and teach

23

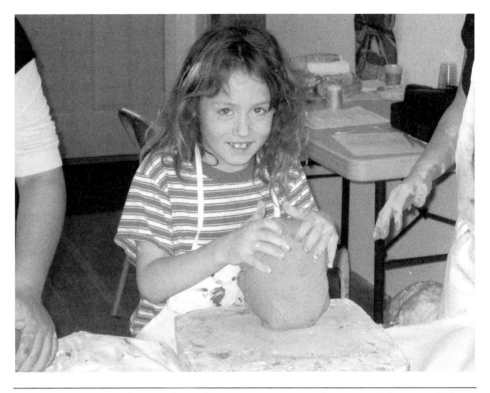

Photo 3.1   A student works on her art project, part of Project ESCAPE, Buhl Arts Council, Buhl, Idaho.

Photo by Kacee O'Connor.

lessons that integrate the arts with the content standards of other subjects and provide access points for parental engagement.

Nonetheless, a trained art educator, artist, or other professional can always be an asset. Moreover, classroom teachers may find that instruction and technical assistance in applying visual arts in the classroom are available, through the district's visual art curriculum specialist; through the professional development center; or from outside, perhaps via a local arts council or museum. Many state arts councils also sponsor summer institutes that provide in-depth training in one or more art forms.

This chapter explores the potential of visual art for curricula integration and parent involvement via several lesson plans and a collaborative project to build a student gallery. The lessons include a project centered around the work of the French artist Matisse, a large-group mural project, and a street painting project that can involve multiple groups of adults and students. These lessons and others that follow in subsequent chapters use a modification of the lesson planning format introduced in the previous chapter.

PROJECT IDEA: MATISSE

Students find value in studying the work of a great artist, gaining information about his or her life and times, responding with works of their own that deal with similar ideas as the artist, and talking with each other about their visual responses. Project Idea 3.1 focuses on Matisse, because the techniques are very accessible to students at most ages.

Project Idea 3.1 | **Matisse**

Subjects

Visual art
English language arts
Social studies

Grade Level

1–8

Purpose or Rationale

Henri Matisse is a major figure in twentieth-century art history. A contemporary of Picasso and the Cubists, Matisse created a way of seeing that was absolutely his own. He helped found the movement known as *Fauvism*—marked by elemental shapes and bold, often unexpected juxtapositions of color—and was a bridge from Post-Impressionism to Abstract Expressionism. His work is alive with visual ideas related to commonplace shapes and objects that surrounded him.

In his later years, Matisse found it physically difficult to paint. He turned to everyday tools, scissors and colored paper, to make his art. Even though he made his paper cutouts with simple tools that anyone can use, many of them are recognized today as outstanding visual works. They use basic art elements like color, shape, and line in new and interesting ways.

The paper cutout method Matisse used (sometimes known as *papier découpé*) provides an excellent medium even for young students, as it requires relatively little formal art training or skill in specialized media.

Content Standards Addressed

- Visual art, including understanding and applications of media, techniques, and processes related to the visual arts, and understanding of the visual arts in relation to history and cultures
- English language arts, including use of listening and speaking skills and strategies for a variety of purposes
- Social studies, especially European history and geography of Africa and the Middle East

Objectives

Understandings

- Art is universally accessible to all of us.
- Some of the greatest art has been done with simple materials.

(Continued)

Project Idea 3.1 (Continued)

- Art is about the world that I see and the world as I see it.
- Artworks can be a pathway for conversations and writing.

Critical Thinking Skills

- Self-knowledge and metacognition
- Sensitivity to context
- Self-evaluation

Materials

- Colored paper: red, blue, green, white, and yellow for starters. Also, purple, pink, and gold are good.
- Large sheets of black paper
- Scissors, glue
- Two to three books or Web sites featuring Matisse paper cutouts. Examples: *A Magical Day With Matisse* (Merberry & Bober, 2002); *Henri Matisse—Drawing With Scissors* (O'Connor & Hartland, 2002)

Grouping or Classroom Modification

During different parts of the project, students work as a full group, in teams, and individually. The classroom should include work tables to accommodate paper cutting and gluing. Space should allow student work to remain undisturbed during stages.

Parent or Family Role

Parents can be involved at various stages, from the initial group discussion in the Artistic Perception stage to the final investigation of career and life connections. They can help students brainstorm ideas for depiction in their cutouts. They may provide invaluable logistical support. For very young children, parents may help them use scissors and glue.

NOTE: This and most other lessons in this book expect that parents will have a major role, often in helping their children with take-home assignments. Teachers who assign these lessons may wish to use a resource such as the TIPS worksheets available from the National Network of Partnership Schools (n.d.). See the Network's Web site, especially http://www.csos.jhu.edu/P2000/tips/TIPSmain.htm. Such worksheets can be modified for subject matter such as the arts.

Procedure

Artistic Perception

Using books, a computer and appropriate Web sites, or color photocopies, show students some examples of Matisse's paper cutouts. Ask them these questions:

- What do you see?
- What kinds of shapes does Matisse use frequently?
- Why do you think Matisse uses the colors he does for each shape?

Have students write their answers in a worksheet or journal. Parent volunteers can become involved in the lesson, working with small groups of students in questioning and discussion.

Historical and Cultural Context

Assign students to teams to conduct research on Matisse and his times. Each team may select a topic such as the following:

- Matisse's influences, including European, African, and Middle Eastern art
- Europe, and especially France, in the early twentieth century
- Matisse's contemporaries, such as Picasso and Miró
- Art movements in the twentieth century, such as Expressionism, Fauvism, and Cubism

Students may elect to present their research in the form of written essays, incorporate findings into artist's journals, or prepare reports that incorporate multimedia. These projects can meet a wide variety of English language arts standards.

Creative Expression

Idea Forming. Lead a session in which you ask students to brainstorm things in their lives that they might depict visually. The students might identify persons or other living things, inanimate objects, or—for older students—abstract ideas and concepts. Write or draw reminders on an overhead transparency as students identify things. Ask students to use sketches and words to make notes. Then, as homework, have them work with their parents to refine their lists.

Individual Work. Follow this with individual student work sessions. Students should first design initial studies with pencils, markers, and paper. Monitor the students' work and offer suggestions (again, this is a good opportunity for parents to help). Guide them with questions:

(Continued)

Project Idea 3.1 (Continued)

- What are you trying to depict?
- Why did you select this color or shape?
- Why are you arranging the different shapes this way?
- What alternatives might you try?

Following their drafts, students should translate their ideas into the cut paper medium.

Aesthetic Valuing

The finished work is assembled for the gallery, which may be a portion of the classroom or some more public space in the school, such as a hall, cafeteria, or auditorium. The process of developing such a dedicated space is addressed later in this chapter. You may want to select some students to be curators. They will have the role of designing the overall exhibition and supervising the hanging of the work. Hold a schoolwide gallery opening, with parents and public invited. Some students may have the role of docents, leading a talk about the work and what it means.

At some point after the work is hung, you should lead the students in a final critique. Use Tool 3.1 to help the students focus on the various stages of art criticism.

Connections, Relationships, Applications

As a finale to the Matisse lesson, engage students in a discussion about art and art careers. Prompt students with these questions: What careers in art and design tap the skills of artists like Matisse? What other ways might drawing and design help you in your life? Students might prepare for the discussion by talking with their parents about careers as designers, artists, or architects. Some parents may actually have such careers and might be invited into the classroom as guest lecturers.

Assessment

Student learning may be assessed via observation of group work processes; critiques of displayed artwork; and ratings of student discussions for participation, extent of contribution, and understanding.

Tool 3.1   Matisse Lesson

This worksheet uses a standard form of art criticism adapted from Anderson (1993). Students should follow the worksheet in order, making notes in each space except for the first.

1	*Perception.* Look at the work without trying to judge it or respond to it. Notice as much as you can. Use this stage to prepare for the next stages, in which you write about what you see. You should spend several minutes just looking.
2	*Description.* Describe the work. Talk about the *visual elements* (shapes, colors, lines, forms, etc.).
3	*Analysis.* Describe how the elements work together. Make inferences about what these visual elements represent.
4	*Interpretation.* Provide your opinions about what the work communicates and how effectively it seems to do this.
5	*Response.* Describe how the work makes you feel (happy, sad, angry, etc.) and why. Don't just say that you like it, but give reasons for your reaction.

From this example of a lesson that involves individual student's artwork, we now turn to two large-group projects. These projects can involve students and parents in the conceptualization and execution of art that is visible and seamlessly tied to the public life of the school and the community.

PROJECT IDEA: A COMMUNITY MURAL

Murals constitute a long tradition in art. From the ancient cultures of the Mediterranean, when fresh paint was applied directly to wet plaster walls in the technique known as *fresco*, the tradition of wall-sized painting has endured. In the first half of the twentieth century, the mural enjoyed a renaissance in

Photo 3.2   In addition to murals, joint art projects can include bead mosaics, such as the Million Bead Project at Moscow Charter School, Moscow, Idaho.

Photo by Jeanne Leffingwell.

Mexico with the muralists Diego Rivera, David Alfaro Siqueiros, and José Clemente Orozco. And in our own time, mural projects have become widespread across the schools of our nation. The artists' directories of many of the state arts councils include muralists who work with schools (examples: Arizona, Idaho, Ohio, Washington state).

Graffiti, which "adorns" many public spaces despite the best efforts of civil authorities, is actually an unstructured form of muraling. By providing a creative outlet for would-be graffitists, murals can create more aesthetic spaces. This example from a school in Arizona shows the power of a mural project on a school:

> The principal said that the walls of buildings one block from the school were covered with graffiti; but at her school the white walls remain pristine, and no one had defaced the school's mural (one child had made a mark on it, but some of the other children made him erase it). There was what she calls a "valuing ethic" which the children carried home from school, creating a community awareness of respect. "We are creating a desire to ameliorate the world with the arts," she said. (Sikes, 1992)

For over two decades, a Chicano muralist named Martin Moreno has worked on school and community mural projects. In various urban, suburban, and rural schools in Arizona, Moreno works with core groups of students to design murals that deal with complex, challenging, and often controversial social issues. The issues are often developed out of surveys of the entire student body. The focus on issues has a direct bearing on these students' lives. Moreno's intent is to help them to think critically about their communities and their lives. In a meeting with the students, he would tell them, "Don't just look at things—start to see! Study. Digest." He tells them, "Many of the negative things of this world come from hate, fear, and ignorance, and the worst is ignorance because it causes the other two." The mural project is a way to learn and defuse negative emotions and limiting thoughts (Sikes, 1992).

Because of its highly public nature, and because it is a large undertaking that may require many hands, a mural is an ideal vehicle for parents and community members to become involved, as advisors, assistants, organizers, and supervisors or team leaders. The preceding examples come from schools that have worked with muralists over time. In rural Idaho, however, another example comes from Northwest Children's Home, which houses children who have characteristically experienced failure and frustration in their relationships and efforts over time. Few of them have had opportunities to build confidence through teamwork and cooperative learning. Using a grant from the state arts commission, artist Will Leaton coordinated a mural on the outside wall of the home to help Northwest's children learn to work collegially and develop social, teamwork, and learning skills. Most of the children at Northwest do not come from the immediate community, so getting community members to become involved in the project might have seemed to be a challenge. A report from the project tells a different tale:

Our school has about 105 kids, all K–12, although this project took place during the summer session, so there were fewer participating. But one of our objectives is to help our kids learn to work together. Ninety percent of our kids are special ed, mostly emotionally disturbed. They have a difficult time forming relationships, particularly with adults. But they were inherently motivated to work on this project. They were eager to help build the platform. They learned teamwork and getting along in a group. Some of the kids, who have the greatest problem with working together, worked with Will in small groups. They held the ladder for each other, helped each other in working, and taking turns. Will was very good at working with them, and they responded with enthusiasm.

One kid who became most involved in the project had never really had any art experience. He became very involved because he was one of our top children and was able to work independently. He soon realized that he had an aptitude for it, that he was creative. He saw the process unfold from the very beginning, building the structure, painting, finishing up, taking care of materials. He went from being a non-artist to being an artist. Although we have no way of knowing what this will lead to, it is obvious he has had a major change.

We are a school that doesn't get the most modern facilities, but the project has had the effect of getting the kids to value their school. Since the project, there has been a noticeable drop-off in graffiti and destruction of property. We had done other projects that were similar, so we expected this to happen, but not to this extent. Then once we got this mural up, it has had a tremendous effect. We got folks from the city, legislators and others, up here. We now have a project going to landscape the entire hillside, to remove some trees that were blocking the mural and to ultimately beautify the whole campus. This will involve the University of Idaho landscape architect, the city forester, and the Rotary. We will have outdoor education using Project Learning Tree for our curriculum. All of this is a result of the project. (Idaho Commission on the Arts, 2005)

These stories demonstrate that murals provide powerful tools for engaging schools and communities. The lesson plan in Project Idea 3.2 outlines the steps necessary for organizing and pursuing a mural project in your own school.

Ultimately, perhaps the process of designing a mural seems too daunting a task for you to take on at the present time. If so, an alternative art project provides all of the public engagement and visibility but without as much of the formality or permanence, as Project Idea 3.2 explains.

Project Idea 3.2 | A Community Mural

Subjects	Grade Level
Visual arts	4–12
Math	

Additional subjects, such as history and science, depending on topic choice

Purpose or Rationale

Part of the reason for the popularity of murals is the scale and scope of the medium. A mural is inherently a large, complex visual work that may involve multiple persons in its design and creation. Because of this, murals are a tool of choice when a school wishes to involve its students in teamwork. Murals have several advantages when they unite students in a joint project:

- A large project, such as a mural, requires coordination, communication, and cooperation—all desirable qualities for students to practice and acquire.
- A mural typically requires the commitment of an extended amount of time, thus allowing students to learn through a process as well as a product.
- The product, and often the process, is large, public, and visible. Murals create student and school pride and signal that the school is a special place. This pride is often shared by the school, community, and neighborhood.
- Murals often deal with themes or ideas that are significant and may even be controversial. Thus they provide a voice to students who might otherwise be unheard and are potentially significant to the community.

Content Standards Addressed

- Visual art, including understanding and application of media, techniques, and processes related to the visual arts, and understanding of the visual arts in relation to history and cultures
- Mathematics, including selection and use of appropriate tools for given measurement situations (e.g., rulers for length, measuring cups for capacity, protractors for angles); other subjects, depending on selected subject or theme (e.g., history)

Objectives

- Students will learn how to work together in a group process.
- Students will develop a complex, extended project that expresses a visual idea.
- Students will gain understanding of a topic relevant to their school or community.

(Continued)

Project Idea 3.2 (Continued)

Materials

- Large sheets of paper or newsprint, for draft sketches
- Pens, markers, rulers
- Paint (preferably acrylic, for ease of cleanup) and painting supplies, donated if possible (contact a paint or hardware store for overruns or mixing errors)

Grouping or Classroom Modification

Regardless of whether the core group comes from one class or multiple classes, there should be scheduling freedom to allow them to work together for extended periods.

Parent or Family Role

Parents should be part of this process from the inception. Parents can help with research, logistics, and some of the heavy work. They should draw upon their own cultural knowledge and experiences, where relevant, to advise students on various stages of the work. While some of their work may come in the form of active volunteering, their input can also be sought through homework assignments in the early design stages.

Procedure

See Tool 3.2 for a helpful planning guide.

Forming the Group

Select the Core Group. Not every student on campus can be part of a mural project. How will they be selected? A core group might consist of a visual art class group, a geography or history class (for an integrated lesson), or a specific grade level. At this point, you may also want to send a mailing to parents to recruit volunteers.

Learn About Murals. You may involve a local arts organization or art museum to provide a visiting presentation on the history of murals, or you might assign research in the library and via the Internet.

Establish a Group Process. Who is the leader? What other roles are there, and who will take them on? How will the group coordinate their efforts and communicate with one another? How will parents be involved? Often a mural project can be supervised by an art teacher—either a school or district art specialist or a visiting artist. This is an excellent opportunity for a museum, especially one that has murals in its collection or staff with expertise, to take a leading role.

Making Aesthetic Decisions

Select a Location. It should be a large wall, ideally visible to all students and visitors through normal foot traffic patterns. In some climates, shelter from inclement weather may be a consideration.

Define the Problem, Issue, or Topic to Be Addressed. Murals usually have a social function, that of communication of a shared idea. What message or idea will the mural convey? As noted previously, a mural's subject may often be challenging and provocative. It is important to have the buy-in of students if the mural is to ultimately have any meaning for them. The following are some possible areas for topic formation:

The School. Since a school is the focus of considerable portions of students' daily lives, the building itself might become a prominent part of the mural, either in the background or as the subject. The school's identity or its accomplishments in academics or athletics may provide visual symbols, such as colors or a mascot.

The Community. The community or neighborhood surrounding the school may also be significant subject matter for the mural, especially if it is connected to the school socially or culturally. The mural might focus on a prominent community landmark, relate a local historical event, or honor the history of a community or ethnic group.

Students. Among the most important actors in the daily life of the school, students are ideal subjects to be depicted in a mural.

Curriculum Areas, Including History, Science, or Math

Developing Ideas. A good way to ignite a mural project is for the team to select a question that guides the work, as in the following examples:

- What problem or challenge does our school or community face?
- What is our vision for the future of the school? How might it look in twenty years, if our vision were realized?
- How is our school connected to its neighborhood or community?
- What metaphors help reveal what our school is (e.g., a *bridge* to the future, a *doorway* toward knowledge, a *journey* of discovery)?

(Continued)

Project Idea 3.2 (Continued)

Develop the Preliminary Design. As a group, you may want to brainstorm what overall visual image or collection of images will portray the problem or deliver the message. Following this brainstorming, students can develop preliminary sketches and paintings on paper.

Begin the Actual Work. This stage will require the greatest amount of time. Parents can be closely involved in all aspects of this stage, doing much of the work, helping with logistics, and providing in-process suggestions for student artists. Preliminary steps may include making any preparations to the surface (e.g., cleaning and priming) to hold the paint; pruning surrounding foliage, or building a scaffold. Students may be assigned specific sections of the space. Math is integrated as they measure dimensions and scale their drawings up to the larger space.

Completing the Project

Although each project is unique, the following outlines the usual steps in completing a mural:

Have Interim Critiques and Coaching. The overseeing artist should check in periodically with the core group to resolve any challenges that are impeding progress and to answer any questions about process or technique.

Hold a Formal Opening to Present the Mural. Parents, civic leaders, community members, and the press should be invited. This could be a fundraising opportunity.

Present and Discuss. At the end of the process, it is vitally important that participants have an opportunity to talk about their work, the process that led to it, and what they learned. Such discussions might take place in public forums, such as a local cable channel, or be part of a feature story for the local newspaper.

Assessment

Student learning can be assessed via observation of group work, rating of individual components of the mural, and evaluation of student critiques and discussions.

Tool 3.2   Mural Planning Timeline

School _____ Project Name _____

Component or Task	Projected Date
Hire resident artist	
Form core team	
Send out mailing to parents	
Select parent volunteers or advisors for project	
Hold organizational meeting; decide on roles	
Conduct research on history of murals	
Develop survey for schoolwide distribution	
Select space	
Distribute survey	
Collect survey	
Make final decisions on subject	
Begin mural	
Complete mural	
Schedule public opening	
Send mailing to parents and press	
Hold public opening	
Hold participant discussion	

Photo 3.3   An I Madonnari street painting festival artist at work.

Photo by Michael Sikes.

PROJECT IDEA: I MADONNARI—
ITALIAN SIDEWALK CHALK PAINTING

I Madonnari is a centuries-old tradition from Italy of drawing or painting images on sidewalks or streets with colored chalk. It derived its name from the Madonna, a favorite subject of the early itinerate painters who often copied old masters, but later, using almost any subject matter became common. Lately, this tradition has been revived in many places in Europe and the United States, notably in Santa Barbara, California, at an annual festival at the local Mission. It can be a powerful group activity that can unite family members (see Project Idea 3.3).

Despite street painting's apparent simplicity, its power should not be underestimated. Each Memorial Day weekend, the 400 selected artists patiently congregate at the old Santa Barbara Mission to begin their work in its deep blacktop. They work, often under a hot sun, throughout the weekend until their painting is done. The event annually draws thousands of visitors who watch the paintings emerge while patronizing food vendors and enjoying entertainment.

Thus far, this chapter has presented several approaches for incorporating visual art into the daily life of the school in ways that are visible and alive for parents and community members. Two of these approaches require no dedicated art spaces, because they are outdoor projects that take advantage of available surfaces. We now turn to a third approach, one that takes up the need for such a devoted space and provides a collaborative process for designing it and making it a reality.

Project Idea 3.3 **I Madonnari**

Subjects

Visual arts

History

Grade Level

2–12

Purpose or Rationale

This project has the advantage of relative simplicity. All you need are colored chalk or oil pastels and a large paved area that people can draw on. The pavement should be relatively smooth, to make the painting easier. (Although technically a drawing medium, this use of chalk is usually called painting because it results in vivid, painterly images.) Blacktop pavement seems to work surprisingly well, as it provides a rich, dark negative space.

Sidewalk paintings are durable enough to be around for awhile if you use oil-based pastels, which also provide a greater intensity of color. Some longevity is important for appreciation and documentation via photography. As weather and shoes take their toll, the images fade away, to be replaced by newer visions the following year.

An I Madonnari is best planned well in advance. Family groups should register ahead of time so that adequate space and supplies are assured. A resident visual artist can be an excellent coordinator for such a project. It can be tied in with a school festival or a fundraiser, such as a Renaissance fair or an Italian street festival.

Content Standards Addressed

- Visual art, including knowing how different media (e.g., oil, watercolor, stone, metal), techniques, and processes are used to communicate ideas, experiences, and stories
- History, including understanding of ways that European society experienced political, economic, and cultural transformations in an age of global intercommunication between 1450 and 1750

Objectives

- Students will be able to work in groups to conceptualize and complete a visual work.
- Students will talk about their work and reflect on its aesthetic qualities.

Materials

- Blocked off section of playground or parking lot
- Chalk or oil pastels

Grouping or Classroom Modification

Students and adults may be paired in a variety of configurations:

1. Nuclear family groups (parents and children)
2. One parent with children from various families
3. Several groups of students with one parent volunteer

Parent or Family Role

The parent's role is integral in this project, either as team member or as supervisor of several students.

(Continued)

Project Idea 3.3 (Continued)

Procedure

The planning and execution of an I Madonnari project logically unfolds in the following stages.

Planning and Recruitment

Initially, you should form a steering committee to coordinate all of the important details. You should identify a space on the school grounds suitable for the project. Develop a mail-out flyer, which can also be sent home via students, to generate interest and to stimulate registration. By the way, registration is critical so that you know how many participants to expect. You may have to cap registration to suit the space available. You might also want to have registrants submit a small drawing of their proposed project and the amount of space they will need.

You may select a theme for the work of all participating teams, or you may leave it up to individual creativity. The latter approach differs from a mural project in providing greater freedom of subject choice. As with the mural project, involve the students in the selection of themes, which may integrate with other curricula in history, science, ecology, or art history. Sidewalk chalk painting can readily be adapted into a formal lesson or unit in which students research the European Renaissance, learn about the growth of art and science, and emulate an artist from that time period in the pavement of the schoolyard.

This is also the time to coordinate the street painting with any other events held on the same day and to plan any refreshments or other amenities you might provide for participants and visitors.

Final Preparations

Nearing the date for the actual event, assign the following tasks and ensure their completion:

- Develop a system for marking off the assigned spaces (e.g., chalk or paint lines), and label each space with the registrants' names.
- Send home a flyer reminding participants to show up on the designated day and to wear old clothes. Chalk gets all over many body parts. Suggest that they bring knee pads (the kind that bricklayers wear, from the hardware store), gardeners' kneelers, or foam pads for protecting knees.
- Make suitable arrangements for publicity and for inviting members of the community.

Celebrate the Artistic Process

On the day of the festival, take lots of photographs of the emerging works for school display and publicity.

Additional information may be obtained from Web sites such as that of the Santa Barbara festival: http://www.imadonnarifestival.com.

Assessment

Students may participate in a shared critique in which they examine their own work. Such a critique can be part of a gallery walk that takes place after the festival day. Students' self-assessments can be recorded as narrative notes or rated via a rubric or scale. Students' research reports related to themes can provide language arts assessment data.

PROJECT IDEA: DESIGNING A GALLERY

Not all visual art can exist as a permanent part of a wall. For much student work, a dedicated display space is necessary. Such a space can be designed by teachers and parents, and the design and construction provide an effective way to involve parents and community members. Project Idea 3.4 provides a process for creating a school art gallery.

Many of the ideas pertaining to visual art are equally applicable to the performing and literary arts. They, too, have demonstrated cognitive value to students and can be integrated across other subjects. They are also capable of powerfully engaging parents and families. They likewise flourish best when dedicated space or facilities are available for their display, performance, and publication.

The next chapter explores the potential of drama and theater for igniting student learning and engaging parents in the lives of their schools.

Photo 3.4   A student displays her artwork, part of Project ESCAPE, Buhl Arts Council in Buhl, Idaho.

Photo by Kacee O'Connor.

Project Idea 3.4 | **Designing a Gallery**

Subjects   **Grade Level**

Visual arts   2–12

English language arts

Mathematics

Purpose or Rationale

No art school, whether an independent institution or an academic department of a college or university, could function without a gallery. This is because the gallery provides the essential context for the display of art, signaling to all who come there that the works therein are special, that they were crafted by hands, minds, and hearts. Whether part of a large museum or a freestanding exhibition space, the gallery provides the home in which the life of visual art is lived. No sensitive person has ever entered the exhibition hall of a gallery or museum and left unaffected.

Having a gallery can teach students many skills not otherwise taught, including presentation, preparation, and conservation of art materials. Curatorship, an art form in itself, flourishes inside the walls of a gallery, as students learn that the placement of objects, explanatory text, and other gallery components constitute the overall meaning of a display.

In view of these advantages, it is surprising that so many schools lack such a dedicated space. Usually, however, it is simply not seen as a priority. Moreover, its absence may reflect a general shortage of available space. However, a workable gallery can be crafted from almost any room or even part of one. All that is needed is some imagination, a good design to use the space that is available, and an understanding of the conditions necessary for effective display of visual work.

Content Standards Addressed

- Visual art standards, especially design arts
- Various standards in English language arts related to oral communication and planning
- Various standards in mathematics, including measurement

Objectives

- Students will be able to conceptualize and design a dedicated space for exhibiting visual artworks.
- Students will develop skills in curatorship, exhibition design, and preparation of artwork for display.

Materials   **Grouping or Classroom Modification**

- Graph paper for designing plans   Students and adults may work in a variety
- Computer spreadsheet software for   of team structures.
  budgeting

Parent or Family Role

Parents have essential roles in planning, design, and implementation.

Procedure

See Tool 3.3 for a helpful planning guide.

Forming the Planning Group

The most important first step is to form a group that sees the importance of a gallery and can work until it becomes a reality. This team can include administrators, teachers, students, and parents or community members. Museum personnel, such as curators and designers, can be excellent partners, advisors, and team members.

The process of designing and building a gallery is so straightforward that the group should be able to get to substantive work with a minimum of preparatory meetings. Thus the formation of the planning group can lead readily to the actual implementation.

Making Decisions

In this decision-making stage, there are three basic steps:

Identify an Available Space. It might be a separate room with no other use or just a part of a larger room with other purposes (e.g., the cafeteria). Even a hallway will do. As long as it provides some permanent place to exhibit two- and three-dimensional work safely and for extended periods of time, any space may prove adaptable, although a hallway or cafeteria make the artwork more visible. Nonetheless, a separate room that can be repurposed has definite advantages: the work may be safer there and it may hold the sense of a dedicated aesthetic space.

Develop a Budget. Some important cost categories include building materials for modifying the existing space, portable partitions for hanging work, display cases or pedestals, and lighting (overhead spots that can be directed to various places work well). Whenever possible, seek the donation of materials from companies in the community. NCLB funds may be appropriate for gallery construction, in view of the parental connection. If school funds are not sufficient, seek an outside grant.

Based on Available Space and Funds, Draft a Design. It should clearly lay out the location of walls for hanging pictures, spaces for display cases, areas for foot traffic and seating, and so on. Build the design into an overall plan that specifies roles, responsibilities, and a timeline for completion.

Completing the Project

Make It Happen. Build the gallery, involving lots of community labor and engagement. After completion, hold a grand opening or an opening exhibition. Use press releases to invite the community. Then continue to use the gallery for rotating displays of exemplary student work and for teaching students the important skills that go with having a gallery of their own, such as conservation, curating, marketing, and publicity.

Assessment

Students may be assessed at multiple stages of this project. In the initial planning stages, designs and collaborative work can be gauged on the use of visual arts elements, the application of effective group processes, and the oral communication of ideas. In later stages, they can be assessed on the degree to which they develop and apply skills in exhibition design, curatorship, and preparation of art for display.

Tool 3.3 Gallery Planning Checklist

Component or Task	✓
Develop an invitation to join a planning committee	
Convene first meeting of planning committee	
Review available space options	
Make final selection of space	
Develop budget	
Develop preliminary designs	
Finalize design	
Schedule construction	
Complete construction	
Curate opening show	
Send invitations and press release	
Hold opening	

4

Developing a Theater Program

Theater is an art form that unlocks what it means to be human. It can reveal the subtle distinctions of character, the complexes of chance and circumstance (what Shakespeare called the "tide in the affairs of men"), and the rich tapestry of human thought and action. It may tap multiple intelligences and channels of expression through the many roles that students and parents can play, not only on the stage but behind it, off to the side, and in front.

Not every school is fortunate enough to have theater on a continuous basis. This chapter presents strategies for tapping community partners and parent volunteers to make the school come alive with this lively art form. As with any other project in this book, you should begin with a vision. Decide what your school would look like if students had broad access to theatrical arts and used them to their fullest potential.

You may need to begin modestly. Use some of the tools, such as the Four-Stage Planning Framework in Chapter 9, to develop a systematic plan. Following the steps outlined in this chapter, you might invite a resident artist or form a partnership with a community theater organization. Build gradually until your program is up and running.

THEATER AS LANGUAGE AND GESTURE

We are all familiar with the power of an actor's voice. It can convey emotion, move forward a plot, and quickly reveal character. But the other major dimension of theater is action, consisting of gesture, position, and movement. An actor must work on both of these aspects, and often the movement must come before the voice. Moreover, persons who never appear onstage (except

45

during preparation)—stage, lighting, and costume designers and directors—are visual artists in their own right. So the visual component of theater is a part of its essence.

The following project starts with the power of language and gradually introduces students to the idea that thought and action are inextricably linked.

PROJECT IDEA: SHAKESPEARE, STUDENTS, AND PARENTS

In *Shakespeare: The Invention of the Human*, critic Harold Bloom (1998) makes the startling pronouncement that William Shakespeare literally recast the modern notion of what it means to be a human being. Through amazing explorations of a range of characters from Othello to Falstaff, Bloom theorizes, Shakespeare provided the models for modern understanding of the human psyche. Even if we do not accept the full implications of this theory, there is no doubt of Shakespeare's enduring genius and seminal role in the formation of the modern mind. That a once obscure actor from a small island, largely off the beaten path of the European Renaissance, should play such a part in the unfolding drama of modern history is surprising.

You can tap this power in the classroom. Shakespeare's more violent plays may be too intense for very young children, and his Early Modern English may be difficult to understand. However, older students will find the vicissitudes of Shakespearian characters consonant with their own life struggles and the richness and power of his language resonant with their own expressive speech. This is a good time to introduce the concepts of poetic language, which Shakespeare amply employed as a vehicle for his plays—both for driving the plot forward and for revealing the sweep and subtlety of character.

In recent days, the online news networks had the following kinds of headlines: "Hurricane Katrina hammers Gulf Coast," "Congress recoils at budget shortfall," "Wall Street at crossroads." Each of these statements expresses a literal truth in nonliteral terms. We usually call such expressions *figures of speech*. They lace our language, and the mass media is not immune to the necessity for their use. Project Idea 4.1 is partially based on this dependency.

PROJECT IDEA: DESIGNING A PERFORMANCE SPACE

By its very design, a school sends powerful signals to those who learn there. Optimally, it tells students that their work is valued and considered important. This is why the creation of a dedicated space for performance is such a critical act. A stage, whether it is a traditional proscenium or an avant-garde black box, creates a new frame of reference. Like a picture frame, it signals that what takes place here is separate from the moments of our daily lives. Between these curtains, it states, magic takes place.

Photo 4.1   A theater artist works with young children.
Photo by Valerie Rhymer.

A theater is a vital, multisensory and interdisciplinary vehicle for student engagement and learning. Through a theater or similar space that can be used as a performance venue, student interest and ability can be nurtured in acting, directing, lighting, set design, dance and movement, music, choreography, and playwriting. The theater thus becomes the pivot for multiple activities that would otherwise be difficult or impossible to attain.

Performance spaces are the arenas in which students unpack and use many of the myriad talents, skills, and aptitudes that are sometimes considered under the general heading of *multiple intelligences*. The following is a sample of the specific performing arts intelligences and the more conventional knowledge dimensions with which they are usually associated:

Acting	Intrapersonal intelligence
Singing	Musical intelligence, fine motor skills
Dance	Bodily-kinesthetic intelligence, gross motor skills
Direction	Interpersonal intelligence
Writing	Verbal-linguistic, interpersonal, intrapersonal intelligences
Technical (lighting, set design, costume, sound)	Visual and spatial, logical-mathematical intelligences

Project Idea 4.1 Shakespeare, Students, and Parents

Subjects

Theater

English language arts

Grade Level

Upper elementary to secondary

Purpose or Rationale

This lesson helps your students write figurative dialogue and then put it into the mouths of characters, who then come alive through their actions.

Content Standards Addressed

This lesson can meet various standards in English language arts (e.g., understanding, identifying, and using metaphor) and theater (e.g., creating improvisations and scripted scenes based on personal experience and heritage).

Objectives

Students will identify and use similes, metaphors, and other figures of speech; students will craft and perform a brief play incorporating figures of speech.

Materials

Resources can be obtained from the Folger Shakespeare Library at www.folger.edu. The National Endowment for the Arts also offers a *Shakespeare in American Communities* learning resource kit available at www.arts.gov.

Grouping or Classroom Modification

The classroom should be set up to allow flexible alternation between group and individual work.

Parent or Family Role

Parents work with students to identify examples of figurative language in contemporary media and participate in small-group work to develop dialogue.

Procedure

Read examples of figures of speech in Shakespeare's poetry or dramatic dialogue (e.g., "All the world's a stage," "Juliet is the sun," "Life's but a walking shadow"). Engage the students in a discussion in which you ask, In what ways is the language not literally "true"? What do we mean by *literally*? Break the word down for them. You may want to read a plot summary of one of Shakespeare's plays to clarify how the figurative speech moves the action forward.

After explaining the concept, present more examples. Then have the students work in small groups to invent their own figurative sayings. This exercise can be carried over into a homework assignment. Ask the students to work with a parent or family member to think of common sayings that are not literally true. Look in the daily newspaper, magazines, or television for examples.

In additional group work in the classroom, have the students select several examples of figurative language and develop characters to say them. They may need to develop additional dialogue around the figures. Then they should write brief narratives of the situation and plot. This can proceed in several stages:

Stage 1. Students create a web or mind map connecting all of the figures of speech that their group has been able to identify, as well as additional dialogue that they wish to include. The teacher and parents can work with the small groups and provide coaching or assistance. Proceeding from the formation of dialogue, the students can next identify several characters and develop ideas about their situations and interrelationships. Key questions to guide this work might include the following:

- What two or three characters do you want to focus on?
- What conflict or life situation are they confronting?
- How are they connected to one another?

Stage 2. Students next can elaborate their ideas by imagining and plotting several connected scenes that carry the action forward. They may develop storyboards that help to graphically illustrate the relationship of one scene to another. This stage may take place over several class periods and include work with parents at home. Students who have no experience acting or who are not particularly comfortable using their kinesthetic intelligence may opt to develop a dramatic reading. Other students, more advanced or sure of themselves, may add gesture and movement to their plays.

Stage 3. In rehearsal and further group work, the students ready their plays for presentation.

Stage 4. The last stage is presentation. Each group should be given the opportunity to present its play. The presentation should include a talkback where the audience (consisting of other class members) engages the actors in a discussion of the meaning of the play.

Assessment

Students can be assessed on their participation in group work and the quality of their plays, including the effectiveness with which they have developed compelling and appropriate examples of figurative speech and incorporated them into dramatic sequences.

Photo 4.2 The Wachovia Playhouse at the ImaginOn in Charlotte, North Carolina.

Photo by Valerie Rhymer.

Theater can be a powerful way to engage children in dance and movement—especially boys, who are often reticent to take advantage of their skills in this area. It can introduce them to grace and athleticism, control and power. The famous sword fight scenes in Romeo and Juliet often provide extraordinary examples of choreography applied to stagecraft. Yet more broadly, learning the techniques of stage movement can gear children up for lifetimes of energy and good health. Activities from drama and theater can meet many of the content standards for physical education (and can help supplement such programs when they have unfortunately been reduced or eliminated).

Performing arts and the spaces in which they happen can be magnets for community involvement. They celebrate the achievement of students, activate community interest, and engage parental volunteerism. All of this becomes possible provided that a space is created in which it can happen. Project Idea 4.2 can guide you through this process.

PROJECT IDEA: A COMMUNITY PLAY

Many regions of the country have historical pageants—plays that depict a significant historic event of the local area. Examples include *The Lost Colony* in Manteo, North Carolina, *Tecumseh* in Chillicothe, Ohio, and many more. At your own school, it is possible to take the traditions of a community and transform them into a work of theater arts. Project Idea 4.3 presents a suggested method.

Many resources can guide you in these steps. The Web even has templates for writing scripts. For example, try Microsoft (http://office.microsoft.com/en-us/templates).

Considering that movement is a vital part of theater leads us to our next art form: dance. As persons who work in schools already know, dance is undiscovered territory. Teachers who journey there will find a different set of challenges, along with opportunities for rich engagement of students and parents.

Project Idea 4.2 | **Designing a Performance Space**

Subjects

Theater

English language arts

Mathematics

Grade Level

2–12

Purpose or Rationale

As with a gallery, a performance space provides the essential context and frame in which the unique works of students can be experienced and more fully understood. The processes of valuing, conceptualizing, and designing a performance space can be as important a part of student learning as the subsequent use of such a space.

Content Standards Addressed

This lesson can meet various standards in English language arts (communicating ideas and following oral and written directions), theater (stagecraft and theater design), and mathematics (measurement, budgeting).

Objectives

- Students will be able to conceptualize and design a dedicated space for performance.
- Students will develop skills in teamwork and cooperative learning.

Materials

- Graph paper for designing plans
- Computer spreadsheet software for budgeting
- Various theatrical equipment (lighting, sound)

Grouping or Classroom Modification

Students and adults may work in a variety of team structures.

Parent or Family Role

Parents will have essential roles in planning, design, and implementation.

Procedure

How to Begin. If the school has an auditorium, all of the elements are in place. Simply beginning to use it as a theater is all that has to happen. However, many schools lack even such elemental facilities. In these schools, the design of a dedicated space is the first step.

As with many projects, a good place to begin might be a residency for a performing artist. This approach could be used with an artist's residency or an interdisciplinary unit with students designing such a space in a school that has no dedicated theater. Although this lesson leads to the design of a black-box theater, other variations might lead toward a more traditional proscenium stage.

Identify an Available Space. Unlike the gallery (see Chapter 3), a performance area should ideally be a separate room with no other use, as demands for space are greater. However, a portion of the cafeteria can be repurposed temporarily. Some additional space, preferably in an adjacent room with a connecting doorway, may be divided into dressing rooms, a makeup room, and a Green Room for actors to wait between scenes. Ideally the performance space should totally lack windows, or the windows should be capable of being completely covered to block out light. Build in space in the theater for technical people (light, sound, video projection) to work. Build space in the Green Room for costume designers or makeup artists to be on hand.

Select a Team. This can include administrators, teachers, and parents or community members. Performing artists or theater personnel can be excellent partners and team members.

Develop a Budget. If school funds are not sufficient, seek an outside grant. Parents and family members can volunteer to secure needed items and materials, often through donations.

Conduct Research. Look into the various forms of theaters, such as proscenium and black box. Possible information sources might include books from theatrical publishers, such as http://www.theaterbooks.com/, or you may contact a local theater company for technical assistance. A visiting artist can also be an invaluable source of information. If space is limited, a black-box theater is preferable.

Based on Available Space and Funds, Draft a Design. It should clearly lay out the location of space for actors (the stage area), seating for audience members, and aisles for people to come and go (including entrance and exit space for actors).

Design Lighting and Sound. Lighting should be adaptable for different plays and should be usable by students, as lighting design is an important theatrical skill. You will need to investigate various options, including the number of lights you will need; the types of lights (e.g., spots, fresnels, ellipsoidals); and any other equipment, such as scrims, gobos, gels, booms, and so on. You might consult a resource book, such as Shelley's (1999) *A Practical Guide to Stage Lighting,* available via online book sellers. The sound system should consist of amplifier, speakers, a control board for using sound creatively, and input devices, such as cassettes or CDs. For all such technical needs, you will need to ensure safe and ample supplies of electrical current at the appropriate wattage and voltage.

Make It Happen. At this point, return to the idea of a residency. A visiting artist not only can help with design of the theater but can spearhead the important final steps that bring it to public life. He or she can work with student talent from play selection through rehearsal and on to opening night. Moreover, a resident artist can help galvanize efforts that might include the generation and distribution of publicity prior to the show and coordinate volunteer actions at the opening.

Assessment

Students can be assessed on the quality of their teamwork and cooperation in designing and executing the overall project.

Project Idea 4.3 A Community Play

Subjects

Theater

English language arts

History, social studies

Grade Level

6–12

Purpose or Rationale

This lesson helps students to understand and value the experiences and knowledge of members of their community by conceptualizing, writing, and performing a play based on local history.

Content Standards Addressed

This lesson can meet various standards in English language arts (conducting research, writing and designing publications), theater (e.g., script writing, directing, acting), and history or social studies (understanding one's local community).

Objectives

- Students will conduct original research into the history of their communities.
- Students will develop skills in all stages of the conceptualization, development, and presentation of a play.

Materials

- Research tools, including video or voice recorders
- Computers and word processors for scripting
- Costumes, props, lighting and sound equipment, materials for set design

Grouping or Classroom Modification

Students and adults will work in both large and small groups and individually in the classroom, in the community (conducting research), and in the theater space.

Parent or Family Role

Parents work with students to conduct research leading to the play and guide students in script writing. Parents can have essential roles as actors and other theatrical personnel.

Procedure

Generate Leadership. Although a wide variety of persons may step up to lead such a project, this is another ideal role for a visiting artist. However, students, teachers, parents, or other community members may also have important roles.

Define the Community. What group or groups of people are the subject of the play?

Conduct Research. Students, often with the help of their parents, may have a prominent role in this stage as collectors of data. Guide your research by asking, What interesting or compelling stories are told by elders (sometimes known as tradition bearers)?

Be Selective. Choose a relatively limited event or series of events, such as one of the following:

- A journey that members of the community undertook
- A challenge that they overcame

About now, start assigning roles: producer, director, writers, technical persons. Selection of actors can come later.

Write a Rough Outline of a Script. Include some sample dialogue. Check to see if it has a feeling of authenticity to those people who lived the experience.

Develop the Script. At this point, you may want to involve a professional writer, preferably a playwright—someone who is able to drive a narrative forward through drama and conflict. This person can help add characters, events, and additional dialogue to your outline.

Start Small. Have auditions with readings of the dialogue. This is a chance to both check out the script and offer actors, both children and adults, opportunities to gain roles.

Schedule the Play and Begin Rehearsals. Set a date for opening night as a goal you must work toward. By this point, multiple copies of the script in finished form should be available. Be sure to allow plenty of time for actors to learn their lines.

Add Scenery, Costumes, Props, Music, Sound Effects, and Lighting. These can be contributed by the various persons assigned to these roles.

Rehearse. Practice until final dress rehearsal. You should establish a detailed schedule for all participants that specifies key dates (e.g., for delivery of props, for lines to be memorized).

Arrange for Publicity. Print invitations. Mail them. Be sure to invite the local newspaper to cover it.

Open Your Play. Enjoy your success.

Hold a Post-Performance Assessment Meeting. Discuss what you have learned and what you might do in the future.

Assessment

Students can be assessed on the quality and completeness of their community research, their collaborative work in the design stages of the play, and their execution of roles in the production.

5

Developing a Dance Program

In 1994, the U.S. Department of Education released its newly developed national standards in the arts, including dance (Kendall & Marzano, 2004). Joe Urschel (1994), a columnist in *USA Today*, penned a sardonic response to the standards, called "Why Johnny Can't Dance." In it, he chortled that the U.S. Education Secretary had a solution for students' woeful reading and math scores—he wanted to teach them to dance!

The columnist had clearly found an easy target. Long consigned to a few weeks in physical education classes, dance has never really been a part of the curriculum. The 1996 National Assessment of Education Progress in the arts found insufficient K–12 dance programs to gain an adequate national sample to assess. Few dance specialists teach in schools, and the classroom teacher that feels confident to try a dance lesson is rare and adventurous.

Yet mounting evidence supports the values of this art form for young people. It increases self-confidence for some students. Like many other art forms, it teaches expression, application, problem solving, and the ability to perform a completed body of work. In an age when child obesity is spiraling out of control—in large part because of children's sedentary lifestyles but also because of endless seat work in reading and math—dance provides a way to reclaim athleticism and channel it in ways that can be fun, meaningful, and productive. Unlike athletics, dance can communicate complex ideas—some that may not be conveyed verbally—making it a complement to English language arts and English language development with exciting potential. And for children who naturally love to move, it can be a hook that excites them about school and learning. Given these advantages, you might want to include a dance program in your school's parent involvement plan.

SHATTERING DANCE STEREOTYPES

Alas, dance advocates face an uphill struggle: dance suffers from the multiple prejudices of elitism (that it is only for a talented few), sexism (that it is not masculine for boys to dance), and irrelevance (that it doesn't develop any skills that are transferable or predictive of later academic or career success). These perceptions guide parents in whether they value dance; conversely, lessons that break down these mythic barriers can help bring parents into the circle of enthusiastic dance supporters and believers. In Washington, a teacher describes this phenomenon at work:

> There are countless examples of parents approaching each other or teachers or the principal to express their support after seeing the impact on their student. A tangible result of this is the unanimous vote, with many supporting comments from parents of past participants, to increase PTA funding for the Discover Dance residency. (Sikes, 2005a, p. 36)

From the same program, a parent says:

> I expected to enjoy watching the kids perform, but I didn't expect to watch the entire performance with a lump in my throat. I was so moved by the opportunity all these children had to be stars—to feel the beauty in the movement of their bodies, to hear the magic of their words, their voices. And to stand on the stage . . .
>
> I've seen a slow awakening of our community to the excitement and physical benefits that dance brings. (Sikes, 2005a, p. 36)

Because of the scarcity of dance teachers in schools, this content area is perfect for an outside artist. He or she may bring a varied repertory of lesson ideas or be able to adapt one of the following lessons. The first project idea, in fact, depends on bringing in a modern dancer from the local community.

PROJECT IDEA: CHOREOGRAPHY WORKSHOP

In a Northwest U.S. community, a traditionally minded father disapproved of his son's enrollment in ballet and refused to attend his recitals; this reticence, however, did not extend to his son's prowess in soccer, of which the father was an enthusiastic fan. On the morning of a dance performance, his son blocked a goal at a soccer game. The astonished man turned to his wife and asked, "Where did he learn how to jump like that?" His wife replied, "The ballet class." That afternoon, the father unexpectedly attended the ballet performance and presented his son with roses.

This anecdote, reported by a Washington teacher, provides the inspiration for Project Idea 5.1, which draws upon the nearly universal human love of sports and athletic skill and their obvious parallels with dance. This lesson incorporates components developed by Deb Brzoska.

In the theater scene in the movie *White Nights*, Mikhail Baryshnikov is talking to a woman colleague. To demonstrate the power of his art form, he executes an extraordinary and challenging dance to Vladimir Visotsky's singing of "Koni Priveredlivye" ("Fastidious Horses"). Toward the end of the piece, the woman's eyes well with tears, demonstrating that sheer movement can engender powerful emotion. You can tap this power in your own classroom, while teaching your students that through the power of their bodies to move through space, they can communicate powerful ideas which they might be otherwise incapable of communicating. Project Idea 5.1 outlines the steps for a choreography workshop.

PROJECT IDEA: TAP

Tap dancing is drumming with your feet. It began with the extraordinary blending of several cultural traditions, including Celtic (Irish step dancing) and African (*juba* from West Africa). Prior to the Civil War, the plantation slaves in the American South were deprived of their drums and prohibited from drumming because their white masters feared the slaves would use drumming to communicate with each other and perhaps plan revolts. The slaves learned to communicate via their tap dancing, thus finding utilitarian and aesthetic uses for this art form. In the twentieth century, tap emerged as a popular form of expression, first among black entertainers in Harlem and later among national audiences through motion pictures. Modern masters of tap have included Gregory Hines and Savion Glover, who blended hip-hop and funk with traditional tap. Project Idea 5.2 gives the steps for a research unit on tap.

The sample projects are only two of many possible ways to bring students into this powerful and kinetic art form. In the next chapter, we move to a discipline that has much in common with dance. In fact, the two have evolved together over the centuries.

Project Idea 5.1 Choreography Workshop

Subjects

Dance

English language arts

Grade Level

Various

Purpose or Rationale

Dance is movement with intention, and the driving force is choreography. While movement is a fundamental human skill, choreography is the planned use of movement through design and notation. (*Notation* in this case means some form of signification. It does not need to be written or particularly formal.) In this lesson, students learn to plan and choreograph motion and to understand that dance is a language with rules and procedures.

Content Standards Addressed

- Dance, including the understanding and use of basic choreographic notation
- English language arts, including comprehension of the sequential nature of composition

Objectives

Working as a group, students will develop a brief dance segment and perform it.

Materials

Photographs or video segments of some of the following:

- Ballet dancers (e.g., *The Nutcracker*)
- Mikhail Baryshnikov in *White Nights*
- Michael Jordan in a mid-court maneuver
- NFL wide receiver catching a pass
- Gymnast, especially during a floor exercise
- Masai warriors
- Native American fancy dancers, round dancers, and so on

Parent or Family Role

Parents work with students in take-home assignments to identify planned or spontaneous movements and record them. Often, they become colearners as their own stereotypes about dance are transformed through careful consideration of the many forms of choreographed movement that we daily celebrate in our mass media.

Procedure

Begin this project by identifying and contacting a modern dancer from the community. Select one who would be willing to lead a class session on body movement. Meet with this guest artist to share ideas and discuss the lesson.

Meeting as a whole group, show photographs (or if possible, video segments) of various examples of movement (see Materials for suggested list). The emphasis in this lesson is not on formal dance but on movement as expression. So as you show these images, ask the students to think about the following:

- What do these images have in common?
- Do you think that each of these people is trying to do the same kinds of things?
- If not, what is different?

Have your students brainstorm words that describe what they see (meets English language arts standards) and write them on an easel pad or overhead. Examples:

- Power
- Speed
- Grace
- Control
- Fluidity
- Self-assurance

At this stage, invite the guest artist into the classroom to work with the students on basic concepts of dance movement. These concepts might include locomotor and axial movements; beginning, middle, and end; and high, middle, and low levels. Then working with the dancer or alone, introduce the word *choreography.* Have the students write it in their worksheets or notebooks. Explain that choreography is planned movement. For example, in the movie *Rocky,* Sylvester Stallone choreographed all of the fight sequences. But ask the students, Do you think that movement in sports is also choreographed? In what ways are specific positions and motions planned ahead of time?

Have the students complete the following homework assignment: Identify a parent, family member, or other adult who has an interest in sports, dance, or some other form of movement. Together, watch an example on television. Discuss how the movements are planned or spontaneous. Look for the movement concepts discovered in class. Using graph paper or a blank sheet, draw a diagram of several representative movements. (Stick figures are OK.) Either with the parent or alone, the student should be encouraged to rehearse the movement.

Back in class, assign the students to teams of three to five each. The teams will brainstorm, using the diagrams they worked on at home, to blend several movements into a sequence. The guest artist can be a valuable resource at this point. Provide time for the groups to practice their sequences. Each team will perform it twice.

After the performances, compare the dance sequences to writing. What similarities do the students see? Can they explain how writing and choreography are both systems of notation that involve the completion of sequences of actions?

Assessment

Students can be assessed on the quality of their group work and the final performance. Each group's performance may be videotaped as an aid to assessment.

Project Idea 5.2 **Tap**

Subjects

Dance

Music

English language arts

Geography

Grade Level

3–12

Purpose or Rationale

Students will study the history of tap and related dance forms as an integrated approach to the cultures of the British Isles, Africa, and the Americas. The focus of this lesson is not on performance but on understanding the cultural forces that make unique art forms possible.

Content Standards Addressed

- Dance, including the history of dance and its connection to world cultures
- Social studies, including European, African, and colonial American history
- English language arts, including narrative and expository writing

Objectives

Students will understand the interconnections of dance, culture, and history.

Materials

- *White Nights* or *Tap,* available for rental or purchase in VHS or DVD
- Computers with Web access
- World maps
- Blank book or binder for Tap Journal

Grouping or Classroom Modification

- Small groups for research

Parent or Family Role

Parents can be partners and team members with their children in conducting research. In addition, they may bring outside expertise into the classroom.

Procedure

Survey your resources to find out how much you or someone else knows about dance history, especially British Isles and African. You may be able to secure a guest artist from a local dance organization or even an amateur folk dance society. Or you may feel secure in your own ability to think on your feet (literally) and lead this lesson, learning while you go. If you have the help of an outside artist, spend a few days planning the exact procedures. The next steps are suggestions:

- Conduct some preliminary research on tap and some of its antecedents, including Irish step dance and West African juba. The library may be a good source, but a Web search should be fine (at the time of publication, Independent Television Service at www.itvs.org was a good source).
- Using one of the videos, show some examples of tap. Ask the students what they see. Make a list of qualities on a chart or overhead. This can prepare the students for their research.
- Have the students conduct research on the origins of tap. At earlier grades, they should be aware that the British Isles and West Africa are primary contributors to this blended art form. In upper grades, they should be able to trace the various routes of immigration and intermingling of the cultures that led to modern tap. This research can meet geography standards.

As a final part of the lesson, students should write an essay or other grade-appropriate written exercise explaining what they have learned.

Assessment

Students can be assessed on their group work, the quality and completeness of their Tap Journals, and their written exercises.

6

Developing a Music Program

Possibly no other art form—in fact, no other content area—has as much potential as music to connect parents to schools, parents to students, students to learning, and one culture to another. Music is accessible at many levels, is universal, and crosses many divides among people. The folk songs played at a Greek or Hispanic festival, the popular music of our parents and their parents before them, the top forty of a rock station, and the offerings of the local symphony orchestra form a rich mélange of rap, salsa, Mozart, heavy metal, big band, country, grunge, and easy listening. People buy music from an industry that has moved in our time from LPs to MP3s and shows no signs of slowing down. People dance to music, sing in the shower, and become enveloped in movie scores.

Given all this, it is not surprising that music is such powerful cultural glue. Schools can tap this richness through a variety of learning experiences that meet standards and engage parents and the community.

Unfortunately, music creates three challenges, which are simultaneously real and a matter of perception. For example, music education requires musical instruments. Moreover, reaching a level of competence sufficient for performance demands hours of student practice. And last, teachers need specialized training or help from trained musicians. Given the absence of music programs in many K–8 schools, the lack of funding to start programs, and the laserlike focus of NCLB on raising scores in English and math, these seem to be daunting challenges.

They don't have to be. This chapter describes processes and provides tools for overcoming these barriers. It includes a project idea for making music that requires no instruments other than some readily available objects. An additional project involves students in a complex investigation of music and world geography.

65

PROJECT IDEA: PERCUSSION WORKSHOP

In downtown Washington, DC, we would often hear the street drummers when we got off the Metro. Mostly African Americans, they would range from boys to young men. A fixture of street corners near the Mall, at Federal Triangle, or at Metro Center, few of them could afford expensive drum sets. Instead, they had ingeniously solved the problem of getting instruments by converting old plastic buckets, usually the five-gallon size. What they lacked in sophisticated equipment they made up in energy and rhythmic virtuosity.

Historically, many drums have been homemade. The first drums were probably carved from trunks of trees. Later, people discovered how to hollow gourds, stretch cowhide over openings, and tap other objects from nature such as cowry shells. Drums expanded into percussion as people learned to strike hollow bamboo or shake dried seed pods. Found objects gave way to increasing technology with the invention of metallurgy and manufacturing.

But the tradition continues into our own time. Around the time of World War II, numerous used oil drums washed up on the shores of West Indies Islands like Trinidad and Tobago or were left there by the military. People of the islands learned how to fashion these containers into musical drums. They were already making the famous steel drums or "pans" that are now a staple of world music, and these large oil drums added to their repertoire of instruments. Successive generations built drums of increasing sophistication, tuned to play a range of notes at various octaves.

You can tap this seemingly universal and innate tendency of people, including children, to create percussion instruments from their environment with Project Idea 6.1. You can scale the lesson to include only simple rhythms or take weeks to encompass complex harmonies.

PROJECT IDEA: A WORLD TAPESTRY OF MUSIC

In the middle 1990s, I was a program officer at the National Endowment for the Arts (NEA) in Washington, DC. Through the doors of the centenary Old Post Office where the NEA is housed, many interesting persons would come, seeking a sympathetic ear for their ideas to use the arts in some new and unique way. Perhaps none was more interesting than Alan Lomax.

Lomax was one of the premier ethnomusicologists of the twentieth century. For decades he traveled over much of the country, recording the folk songs, blues, bluegrass, and gospel of sharecroppers, laborers, men on chain gangs, and people in prison. His recordings constitute a priceless repository of the experiences and dreams of ordinary people. On this occasion, late in his life, he had come to the NEA to demonstrate an extraordinary idea called the Global JukeBox. It would use multimedia to catalog the world's music and cross-index it to other ethnographic information about world cultures. Lomax had long ago formulated the vision, but it took technology until 1995 to catch up with him.

Although multimedia corporations and the National Science Foundation initially supported his idea, it languished through the 1990s. Alan Lomax died in 2002, but his work and his vision live on.

Today, in this age of iPods, MP3s, and digital music, that vision is readily obtainable. You can take the same concept and make it come alive in your classroom, using Project Idea 6.2.

From music, we turn to one final art form, that of literature and creative writing.

Project Idea 6.1 **Percussion Workshop**

Subjects	**Grade Level**
Music	K–8
English language arts	
Math	

Purpose or Rationale

Students learn about the history of drums and percussion instruments while constructing their own homemade instruments and performing in a concert.

Content Standards Addressed

- Music, including the history of world music
- Math, including the use of measurement and geometry for three-dimensional design
- English language arts, including listening skills and writing descriptive texts
- Social studies, especially the study of world cultures

Objectives

Students will understand that musical instruments reflect the needs and resources of people across the world.

Materials

- Various books, Web sites, and CDs on percussion, drums, and pans
- Objects that can be struck or converted to percussion instruments
- Materials for construction

Grouping or Classroom Modification

Students work in a large group, then in various groupings with parents. Performance is grouped according to instrument type.

Parent or Family Role

Depending on their comfort level, parents may be involved in the design of the homemade drums. They will help locate an object—from a list generated in class—that can be repurposed. Parents can help in design (aligning with mathematics standards), drawing a schematic of the drum with the measurements. Their success in doing this will vary from one parent to another. Absolute standards of quality are not so important as their interest and enthusiastic involvement in the project.

Procedure

Begin the lesson by introducing the history of drums and percussion. Accessing resources from books and the Web, show pictures of different early and historic drums. Play examples from CDs to illustrate sounds.

Explain how drums and percussion instruments can be homemade. Demonstrate with some objects of your own. How many things in the home can make a sound when tapped or struck? Make a list on an overhead transparency. Examples: plastic tubs or buckets, coffee cans, bamboo pieces from fishing poles (when hung with strings), glass jars, metal tubes.

Design. You can either send a sign-up sheet home to enlist parents as volunteers for a musical instrument workshop (for which you will need a dedicated space) or have each student work with a parent or family member on an individual instrument. This will vary with individual parents. If one parent has special expertise (as a drummer, for example), he or she might help lead the workshop and mentor other adults.

Completion of Designs. These should be drawings with accurate and precise measurements and lists of raw materials and tools. Also have available step-by-step written descriptions of how to assemble the instruments (meets English language arts standards). The degree of difficulty and safety issues should be carefully addressed and reviewed for appropriateness and skill levels of both students and adults. See Tool 6.1, Music Instrument Design Template.

Assembly. Complete assembly of the instruments as a home assignment. Allow two to three days, with interim progress reviews in class, or do as a part-day workshop at school.

Rehearsal or Practice. Get the class together and divide into groups, based on instrument types. Start with basic, simple rhythm patterns modeled after examples from one of the books or CDs, possibly using a brief excerpt that the students can play along with. You will not need musical notation but should have the students practice until they memorize their patterns. In this stage, you have a number of options for helping the class decide on the structure of the music they are developing:

- Decide on the number of measures required of each group.
- Decide whether the rhythm patterns are to be played separately in sequence, together in groups of instrument types, all together as a group, or in some other combination.
- Decide how many times each pattern should be repeated.
- Decide whether the various repetitions should be played at the same dynamic level or if the dynamics should change in some way.

Have each group of students outline their piece in words or icons so that they can memorize the format for the performance. Later, improvisation can be added; initially, however, it is important for the students to work toward a unified effect.

Performance. A percussion festival can encompass the whole school and feature a performance by the students and a photo exhibition documenting the design and production of the instruments. Or you may have an invitation-only performance with parents in the classroom.

Assessment

Students can be assessed on the clarity and accuracy of their designs. The written descriptions and specifications can provide assessment of English language arts. Math, especially measurement, can be assessed through an analysis of the designs and their application of mathematical principles. In addition, you may wish to develop a rubric for assessing various musical standards, including performing, responding, and critically analyzing the performances of others. Depending on the students' ages, they may be able to help develop a rubric. The ability of each group to work together can provide valuable assessment of group work and cooperative learning skills.

Tool 6.1 Music Instrument Design Template

Student name: _____

Parent or adult: _____

Type of instrument (e.g., drum, xylophone, miscellaneous percussion):

List of needed materials:

List of tools:

Draw diagram here and include precise measurements for each part of the instrument:

Project Idea 6.2 **A World Tapestry of Music**

Subjects	**Grade Level**
Music	All
English language arts	
Social studies	

Purpose or Rationale

In this lesson, students learn that music is a pathway to knowledge of lands and cultures. The lesson can be extended into a unit that takes place over several months and integrates with various subject areas.

Content Standards Addressed

- Music, including world music history and ethnomusicology
- English language arts
- Social studies, especially the study of world cultures

Objectives

Understandings

- Music is a vast global tapestry of sounds.
- Although it comes in many flavors, it generally serves the same purpose in all lands and among all peoples.
- Even though it has regional origins, it all belongs to everyone.

Knowledge and Skills

- Students locate regions on a map, showing where their ancestors came from, if they know this information. Students who do not know their place of ancestry can choose a region that particularly interests them.
- Students find music that comes from their place of origin, ancestry, or interest as well as those of their classmates.
- Students explain differences and similarities among world music.

Materials

- Computer with Internet connection and speakers
- Audio playback devices: CD player, iPod, and so on

Grouping or Classroom Modification

Students will need to work together as a large group and in pairs or small groups.

(Continued)

Project Idea 6.2 (Continued)

- MP3 or CD samples of music,
  available from sites such as
    www.apple.com
    www.itunes.com
    www.music.com
    www.mindawn.com
    www.magnatune.com
- World maps, 3×5 cards

Parent or Family Role

Parents can help students to identify examples of music from their own cultures or cultures in which they are interested. Such examples can be used in the classroom components of the lesson.

Procedure

Select examples of music from different parts of the world (your librarian or media specialist should be able to help you) and play them for the class. Brainstorm with the students: What do they hear in the different selections? Where do they think that each selection comes from? What reasons do they have for their thinking? You may want to work with the students in putting the collected pieces into categories based on their function—marches, lullabies, work songs, special occasion music, and so on—and then compare the music across cultures. To what extent is all the music in a use category the same across cultures?

As a take-home assignment, have the students work with parents or family member to identify some music from a CD, MP3, radio station, or television. It might be music that is related to their cultural heritage. If possible, the students are to record a part of the music and bring it to class.

On a large map of the world, have the students work in pairs to make 3×5 cards identifying each music sample and placing it on the appropriate part of the map. They may also conduct additional research and record anything else they can learn about the country and region.

From here, the lesson can be expanded as a framework for studying geography (maps, countries, regions), history (migrations and national origins), English language arts (students' descriptive narratives of place), and science (earth science and biology). The potential for such expanded units is constrained only by the targeted standards.

Assessment

At a basic level, students can be assessed on their identification of music samples and countries. Additional expansions of the lesson or unit can involve written and performance-based assessments in other subject areas.

7

Developing a Literary Arts Program

Of all the treasures we have transported across the ages, language may be the most powerful, closely guarded and sacred. It is the doorway of opportunity, the well of our shared knowledge. From the first cooing we hear at birth to the prayer whispered at our deathbed, language is the silken thread we follow through the labyrinth that is our life.

"The pen is mightier than the sword," Bulwer-Lytton famously remarked, and characters real or fancied from Marc Anthony (in the famous funeral oration that incited the fury of the Romans) to Churchill (who stiffened Britain's resolve against the fury of the Third Reich) have understood this. In modern times, masters of literature and oration have leveraged history, perhaps none more famous than Martin Luther King, who faced an audience of a quarter of a million people on the Washington Mall and summoned them to imagine a future of mutual respect and equality.

So language is power. But language can also be lifeless and flat. And it is this difference between the powerful and the prosaic that constitutes the main focus of this chapter. It is a critical difference in this time of high-stakes accountability. This is because language arts are already a major focus; in fact they are *the* major focus in the school day, because of the literacy emphasis of NCLB. This is generally a positive step since it places language at the forefront of education and raises the bar for schools and students.

All too often, however, the programs fostered under this legislation ignore creative writing or treat it as only a functional skill. In fact, much of the writing instruction in America's schools is probably unequal and inconsistent. But in these respects the instruction, and the textbooks from major publishers, can be no better than the standards that they follow. And we can be certain that the primary authors of the standards were not poets. A list of some of the things that the standards do not cover sounds like a poet's toolbox: passion, commitment, emotion, inflection, cadence, intonation, posture, eye contact, and gestures. This list of authors' tools, many of which may be used in the written as well as the spoken word, is the subject of the next project idea.

PROJECT IDEA: SLAM POETRY

In the time of Wordsworth and Coleridge, poetry was the preeminent medium. Through the nineteenth century, people turned to their poets for stimulation, excitement, and the deep insight into life that this writing could provide. The poet laureate of Great Britain was a national hero. A book of Elizabeth Browning's sonnets was the equivalent of today's summer blockbuster movie. The Victorian Era represented the high point in the evolution of poetry as a public medium, enjoyed by both the aristocratic and the humble. But in our own time, poetry has sought refuge in the libraries of scholars and the classrooms of English departments, no longer a thing of much interest in the world market of ideas.

Yet poetry has been reclaimed by some unexpected champions. The writers of popular songs in a wide variety of genres—rock, folk, bluegrass, blues—have continued to put words to meter and rhythm, in a sense taking poetry back to its roots. Because long before printing, poetry had been a primarily oral medium—typically sung rather than spoken in monotone—and it had a history well back to Gilgamesh, the Sumerian hero epic sung by countless tongues and written down in wedge-shaped cuneiform.

This oral tradition is resurrected in both rap and slam poetry. In Project Idea 7.1, these traditions, ancient and modern, are fused in a lesson that unleashes the power of children's words.

Through school programs energized by poets, writers, and literary organizations, *literacy* can become *creative writing.*

PROJECT IDEA: COMMUNITY WRITING PROJECT

This kind of project can involve students in researching and writing about their families, local history, or any of a hundred things that are rich, engaging, and unique to a local area. It can begin with some of the same research tools used in other lessons and activities, although often the research may initially be more of an individual nature rather than a group effort. Project Idea 7.2 outlines the steps.

This project can also lead into the design of a student-parent literary magazine.

Project Idea 7.1 Slam Poetry

Subjects

English language arts

Grade Level

6–12

Purpose or Rationale

Students learn to connect their own power of expression with the main currents of poetry and personally reclaim their access to an ancient art form.

Content Standards Addressed

English language arts, including the composition of poetry and the use of spoken language conventions

Objectives

Students will compose their own poems and perform them.

Materials

Poetry selections characterized by robust oral qualities (e.g., various Shakespeare soliloquies; *The Congo,* by Vachel Lindsay; *Do Not Go Gentle Into That Good Night,* Dylan Thomas; *Dream Deferred,* Langston Hughes; *You're Blind,* Run DMC). Also, check out slam poetry podcasts or downloads (do a search) for other rap and hip-hop examples.

Grouping or Classroom Modification

Whole class, team, and individual work

Parent or Family Role

Parents have several roles in this project. They may help their students in idea formation and even serve as coauthors during early drafts. If they are able to come to the classroom, they can also be critics, judges, and audience members.

Procedure

Read some poetry selections to the class. Then guide a discussion through the following questions: What did they notice? In what ways is poetry different from ordinary, everyday speech? Can they think of examples from modern entertainment that are similar to these poems?

Assign the students to think of a subject for a poem. It should be something they care about. They may work with a parent or other adult at home to develop some ideas. Devote several classroom sessions to developing the poems, with prewriting, successive drafts, and editing.

You may want to divide the students into teams to work on their poems. On the day of the performance, you can have a poetry "slam," with teams competing. As with adult poetry slams, members of the audience can be the judges.

Assessment

Students can be assessed on the quality of their participation in all stages of the writing process and the quality of their own poems in terms of forcefulness, vigor, and clarity.

Project Idea 7.2 Community Writing Project

Subjects

English language arts

English language development

Various other subjects, depending on writing focus

Grade Level

2–12

Purpose or Rationale

Writing is best when it is purposeful and is approached as a multistage process. This means that students will do their best work when they choose a topic of interest and are guided through successive stages of idea formation, writing drafts, editing, refining, and publication.

Content Standards Addressed

- English language arts and English language development, specifically writing
- Various standards in science or history/social studies, depending on student selections of writing topics

Objectives

- Students will identify writing topics that interest them and that are appropriate, based on significance or relevance to their community.
- Students will complete the various stages of writing.

Materials

Computers, printers

Grouping or Classroom Modification

Students work together in full-classroom grouping and individually.

Parent or Family Role

Parents can have significant roles as providers of information that may inform student research.

Procedure

As with any research, this writing project unfolds in several stages:

Research. Find out about some aspect of your town, community, or neighborhood—its environment, culture, or history.

Begin to Narrow. Identify a topic, question, problem, hypothesis, or just an interesting anecdote.

Brainstorm Ideas as a Group. This helps each writer to begin to focus.

Write Initial Drafts. These are often just the first of numerous drafts as writers refine their craft. An editor (often the teacher) should provide continuous feedback on multiple versions of each piece of writing.

Finalize. Ensure that each work is perfect in form, content, and grammar. Print them out. They can be bound as a book for sale or donation.

Assessment

Students can be assessed on their writing at each stage, using rubrics or rating scales that are widely available through the state's content frameworks for English language arts. Students may also be assessed on their treatment of knowledge from other content areas as writing topics.

PROJECT IDEA: STARTING A LITERARY MAGAZINE

Elsewhere we have seen the power of dedicated spaces for the arts: a gallery to frame visual works, a theater to frame drama. In a sense, literary art also needs a frame—a distinctive surround that deservedly sets the work off from commonplace experience while making it more accessible. That frame is usually some form of publication.

Creating a literary magazine or journal to feature student work can ensure that student work is read more widely on campus, and it can also move it out into the community and into the hands of parents.

Creating such a publication need not be daunting. Naturally, a visiting poet or writer can be very helpful in overcoming some of the technical challenges. Moreover, parents and community members who make their living in the publication or graphic fields can be invaluable sources of expertise and needed resources.

Student publishing can be augmented by reading nights at the school with parents attending to enjoy recitations by their children of their own work.

PUTTING SEVERAL ARTS TOGETHER

Once you have established even a beginning program in one art form, you may want to try putting arts disciplines together. The possibilities are limitless. So consider each of the preceding chapters, which for clarity focus on single arts forms, as starting points for experimentation with a wide variety of blending and cross-fertilization.

In the next chapter, we move from a focus on individual arts forms and disciplines to an interdisciplinary approach centered around the authentic contexts of home, family, culture, and sense of place.

Project Idea 7.3 Starting a Literary Magazine

Subjects

English language arts

Visual arts

Grade Level

6–12

Purpose or Rationale

Elsewhere we have seen the power of dedicated spaces for the arts: a gallery to frame visual works, a theater to frame drama. In a sense, literary art also needs a frame—a distinctive surround that deservedly sets the work off from commonplace experience while making it more accessible. That frame is usually some form of publication.

Creating a literary magazine or journal to feature student work can ensure that student work is read more widely on campus, and it can also move it out into the community and into the hands of parents.

Creating such a publication need not be daunting. Naturally, a visiting poet or writer can be very helpful in overcoming some of the technical challenges. Moreover, parents and community members who make their living in the publication or graphic fields can be invaluable sources of expertise and needed resources.

Content Standards Addressed

- English language arts, including writing in various genres
- Visual arts, especially graphic design

Objectives

- Students will write original compositions and revise them through successive drafts until final publication.
- Students will produce a publication that integrates literature and graphic design.

Materials

- Computers with dedicated file storage and software
- Printer
- Printing paper, cover stock, and binding

Grouping or Classroom Modification

Students will work in small groups and individually.

Parent or Family Role

Parents can be invaluable partners at all stages in the development of a literary magazine. They may help set up the dedicated space and equipment, jury selections for each issue, secure donated services or supplies, and distribute the magazine in the community.

Procedure

Any periodical needs to have a home. At a minimum, you should secure several computers that are available often enough for students to input and edit their work. The computer lab is an excellent candidate for this role. (A dedicated space might be ideal but is not absolutely essential.) You should ensure adequate and safe file storage space, preferably on a dedicated hard drive, for student work.

You will also need software. Although word processing programs such as Microsoft Word or WordPerfect are good at what they do, their capabilities don't really extend to laying out and formatting a publication that will appear in multiple editions. Choose a page layout program, such as Microsoft Publisher, Quark Express, or Adobe InDesign. Steep educational discounts are available from qualified vendors.

You will also need a printer, preferably a fast and high-quality color inkjet or laser printer.

You may want to form a committee or staff that includes students and parents, with one or more faculty advisors. In its initial meetings, this committee can make important decisions such as the name of the magazine and its focus. Will it publish only short stories and poetry or also include nonfiction? Will it accept student photography or other artwork? Subsequent work of this committee may include appointment of key roles: editor, associate or assistant editors, graphic designers, and possibly a circulation manager to supervise the work of selling subscriptions.

Although you may print your journal onsite, you may have to go off campus for binding. You might approach a local printer to donate binding materials and services in exchange for a complimentary advertisement in the journal.

The publication of the journal can be augmented by reading nights at the school with parents attending to enjoy recitations by their children of their own work.

Assessment

Students who submit work to the journal can be assessed on the quality of their writing. Those students who work as staff members can be assessed on their use of editing and revision skills. All students who work on the journal can be assessed on their collaborative and group work.

8

Developing a Folk and Traditional Arts Program

In the late nineteenth and early twentieth centuries, a great river of immigrants—most of them from Europe—flowed through Ellis Island and then into America's burgeoning cities; from there, these waves often broke into rivulets and flowed into the small towns and vast prairies of the Heartland.

In those years, the role of the U.S. school, in addition to teaching knowledge, was the transmission of the ideas and values that made the nation what it was—freedom, mobility, loyalty, industry. Education was the engine of assimilation for immigrants eager to shed the raiment of their previous lives and proudly become Americans. Through education, they and their children could learn the language and the ways of their new home. The school was the stove that kept the American melting pot at a full boil.

Today, the melting pot has given way to the rich stew whose various ingredients retain much of their individuality while contributing to the piquant flavor of the whole. Part of the reason for this is that new waves have come to our shores from new and distant places: Hmong in Washington, DC; Somali in Columbus, Ohio; and Salvadorians in Charlotte, North Carolina, have defied the old ethnic patterns and chosen to retain their identities. And they have joined people who have been here longer than the white, Anglo "majority": Nez Perce in Idaho; Navajo, Hopi, and Spanish Americans in Northern Arizona; and Native Hawaiians in Hawaii, among many other examples.

While the values that have been honored and celebrated have not changed—children still recite the pledge, commemorate Thanksgiving, and study the lives of great countrymen and women—those observations and lessons frequently involve children of many colors, languages, accents, and lifeways. Though the imperative to learn English at a high level is even more essential than ever to these students' success, English lessons may draw upon a wealth of native languages and home cultures for their successful acculturation.

To function effectively in these new times and to prepare all students for a world their parents never knew, schools must recognize, embrace, and internalize diversity. The way that schools will do this is not through science or math, which are much the same across nations and peoples. Nor do the standards for history and social studies allow much leeway for multicultural studies, since they focus entire school years on state and national history. Instead, it is primarily through the visual, performing, and literary arts that internalization can happen.

A CULTURAL FESTIVAL

Throughout the country, communities set aside a part of their summer to acknowledge their roots through cultural festivals and celebrations. This acknowledgement of diversity seems to be part of our national character. Moreover, it takes place in communities large and small: Milwaukee has its Summerfest, with successive celebrations of its African, German, Irish, Italian, Latin, and Polish heritage. Santa Barbara commemorates its French, Italian, Greek, and Latino roots. These festivals provide a useful model for schools.

You can compress a summer's worth of festival into a few days with a simultaneous celebration of all the cultures in your school. In the process, you can encompass multiple arts forms and bring in activities and objects that are sometimes marginalized and excluded from the fine arts: crafts, cooking, dress, traditional occupations, such as farming and trades, and so on. In fact, there's no reason to separate these out, since they are part of what gives cultures their individuality.

Just what is possible in a cultural festival is illustrated in the following remembrance:

Festa! Italiana: Milwaukee's Italian Cultural Festival

We often schedule a visit to my wife's family in Milwaukee during Festa! Italiana, the city's summer festival honoring its Italian roots. On the day we go, we feel excitement as we park down by the harbor and walk through the entrance to the fairgrounds. Everywhere, there is food—pasta, fried calamari, and especially pizza, including the thick, bready, Sicilian *sfincione*. As we *passagiamo* through the grounds, we hear strains of old standards in Frank Sinatra and Connie Francis style from the bandstands. We *mangiamo* on pizza, stop to kiss cousins and aunts, reminisce with my wife's former music teachers, and greet friends not seen since last year. We watch children perform folk dances, followed by a troupe of extraordinary *Calendimaggio* flag throwers from Italy.

> Cousin Dominic has a tent with his lifetime collection of opera; multiple headphones allow you to listen to Caruso or Renata Tebaldi sing *Pagliacci.* (What is more Italian than opera?) But elsewhere, "modern" music plays. (Well, Jerry Vale—not really modern, but from our parents' day.) Tents house photo displays depicting the old Third Ward neighborhood—grocery stores, street scenes, and innumerable weddings.

This extraordinary panoply of images, sounds, and cooking could not have taken place without families and people of the community. This would also be true in a school festival; it could not happen without drawing parents in.

"A great idea," you may think. "But it probably takes months of planning." In fact, a comprehensive, citywide festival probably takes year-round planning. But your Festa doesn't need to take up a fairground or run all summer. It can be planned by a committee and realized through volunteers, school staff, and students. And it can include a lesson or unit that meets standards in several subject areas.

If this is your first foray into the realm of cultural festivals, you may have no idea how to begin. The answer, not only for this project but for most of the ideas in this book, is to get some help. Begin discussing the idea in order to stimulate energy and engagement from others. With their help, you should be able

Photo 8.1   Folk dancers performing at Milwaukee's summer Italian festival, Festa!

Photo by Laurie Sedlmeier.

to build enough interest to form a small committee. If you are lucky enough to already have some parents intrigued with the idea, involve them right away. Have a meeting and brainstorm some ideas. Use some of the questions in the following planning guide, Tool 8.1, to frame your discussion.

From this initial meeting, it is a natural process to develop a flyer or letter and send it to your students' parents. You might be able to use local organizations as intermediaries. Find some partners in the communities and neighborhoods you want to reach. In this early stage of planning and communication, you also need to develop a timeline, using a planning template such as the Cultural Festival Planning Framework in Tool 8.2.

In the intermediate planning stages, you need to have each potential participant answer these questions: What is my role? What will I bring? Where will it be located in the school? What hours or days will I be there? (This will depend on the master schedule for the festival. Saturday may be a good choice.) Will I present, perform, or demonstrate?

As you approach the day of the festival, the school should take on the aspect of a very busy place. People should be putting up displays, setting spaces for demonstrations, and rehearsing performances.

On the day of your festival, you should have a broad cross-section of the community attending, including the media. This is a great opportunity to continue the momentum you have built up.

A useful source of information and ideas for using folklore in schools is the Smithsonian Institution and its Folklife Festival. This annual celebration takes place in the summer on the Mall in Washington, DC. Information on this event, and many of the tools and resources you can derive from it, are available online at http://www.folklife.si.edu/index.html. (This URL is for the Smithsonian Center for Folklife and Cultural Heritage. It links directly to the information on the Festival.)

PROJECT IDEA: WRITING ABOUT CULTURE

As a part of this cultural festival as an overall school project, teachers may elect to teach the lesson described in Project Idea 8.1, which meets national and state standards in English language arts and English language development.

As an ongoing practice, the arts can be a doorway to all streets and avenues of the community. The festival galvanizes, but the arts activities that take place throughout this book are designed to celebrate the broadest and richest diversity that stands outside—and increasingly permeates—the school's gates.

Further Reading

In addition to the Smithsonian site, numerous resources await your exploration as you enrich your knowledge of multicultural education. They include the National Association for Multicultural Education (http://www.nameorg.org/) and the University of California Graduate School of Education's Responsive Learning Communities page (http://www-gse.berkeley.edu/research/rlc/index .html).

From the concept of multiculturalism, we move next to a set of projects specifically designed to uncover and engage the traditional arts that reside in your neighborhoods and families.

Tool 8.1   Cultural Festival Initial Meeting Planning Guide

Questions

How many different cultures are represented in our school? Who are they?

What time of year should we select for the festival?

How large a festival do we want to have (e.g., whole school or selected rooms)?

Who else do we need on the team?

What are the assignments and roles?

How will we identify and contact a diverse range of parents? (This is a critical next step.)

Tool 8.2   Cultural Festival Planning Framework

Task	Date
Identify parent groups that might become involved.	
Send out flyers to parents.	
Make contact with interested parents.	
Form a planning committee and hold first planning meeting.	
Hold second planning meeting.	
Send out community invitations and publicity.	
Check interim progress.	
One week from festival, conduct walk-through of site.	
Ensure that logistics are in place.	
Hold the festival and celebrate.	

Project Idea 8.1 **Writing About Culture**

Subjects

English language arts

Grade Level

Multiple

Purpose or Rationale

This lesson introduces students to the idea that their own cultural heritages are valuable and to be appreciated. They learn how to celebrate them by writing about them. The writing involves learning about them through research, possibly including family ethnography.

Content Standards Addressed

This lesson can meet various English language arts standards, especially in areas of investigation, research, and writing.

Objectives

Students will understand that their cultural heritages are complex, interconnected weaving and that they have an active role in their continuation. They will also come to see them as irreplaceable gifts that they actively value and celebrate.

Students will be able to identify compelling questions about their cultural heritages: Where did we come from? Why and how did we come here? What makes us unique? How have our people lived? What do they think? What do they value?

Materials

Various writing materials

Grouping or Classroom Modification

Individual or group work

Parent or Family Role

Parents and other family members, and especially elders, are the priceless sources of information and remembrance that make this project happen.

Procedure

Start with a brief discussion. What is culture? Look for examples. Help students sort examples from nonexamples. A good working definition will include objects people value over time, rituals that give meaning to life, and so on. Brainstorm the questions and decide on the most useful answer.

Give students the following assignment: Based on the question, find out about your family's culture. Select a research method (or more than one):

- Documentary research, which may include examination of family letters, photos, home videos, and other artifacts
- Written accounts and records
- Interviews with family members

Write an essay based on what you find.

Student works can be presented as literary journals, bound books, a display in the cultural festival, or readings, as in a bookstore.

Assessment

Students can be assessed on their participation in group discussions and the quality of their research, writing, and presentations.

TAPPING YOUR COMMUNITY'S TRADITIONS

Folk arts, folklife, and *folklore* are varied terms for the fibers and strands of tradition and meaning that connect people to one another, to places, to objects, and to activities that tend to be repeated over the years. These traditions are vital in that they give people a sense of identity and belonging, while conveying and transporting values across time.

Because of their intimate connections with families and communities, folk arts are powerful linkages for parent involvement in schools. They have the advantages of respecting what comes directly from people's lives without placing a premium on judgments of artistic merit or talent.

The following section explores various options for tapping these intrinsic strands of meaning that already run deep in communities. It outlines approaches that can originate with a single artist's residency or classroom project and can lead to deep and lasting partnerships between a school and its community. It begins with a relatively simple lesson in which students get a clearer picture of the places they call home.

Photo 8.2   Artists work on a traditional arts project.

Photo by Jeanne Leffingwell.

PROJECT IDEA: MAPPING THE NEIGHBORHOOD

Project Idea 8.2 is meant for older students. This exercise is treated as a research project with three distinct stages.

Project Idea 8.2 **Mapping the Neighborhood**

Subjects	**Grade Level**
English language arts	6–12
History/Social studies	
Visual art	

Purpose or Rationale

This lesson gives students the opportunity to explore their own neighborhoods and begin to understand what they are like as places.

Content Standards Addressed

- English language arts, including writing and speaking
- History/social studies, including the knowledge of local communities
- Visual art, including the selection of materials and processes for two-dimensional drawing

Objectives

Students will understand that neighborhoods are complex entities with individual characteristics that reflect the people who live there.

Materials	**Grouping or Classroom Modification**
C.A.R.T.S., Sample Parent Workshop: "Exploring Your Neighborhood," from www.carts.org or school_bparent.html	Students can work as a full group, in small groups, and individually.

Parent or Family Role

Parents are involved as collaborators in planning, mapping, and interpretation.

Procedure

Stage 1: Planning

Introduce the concept of *neighborhood,* discussing the characteristics of neighborhoods and how they are usually defined. On an overhead, draw a rough map of the area that surrounds the school. Then have the students form teams based on their neighborhoods. You might use a map and their addresses to help them pair up. In teams, have them begin to draw maps of their neighborhoods.

(Continued)

Project Idea 8.2 (Continued)

As homework, ask the students to work with family members to plan a trip through their neighborhood. This can be a group activity but needs at least two people. Decide on which parts of the neighborhood to walk and which parts to drive. For all but the oldest of students, of course, an adult needs to be along to drive and supervise.

Stage 2: Data Collection

While traveling through their neighborhoods, students should collect information on the following elements, using a combination of descriptive and statistical methods, including at a minimum a narration, lists, and a diagram:

- Dwellings: single-family homes, condos, apartments, mobile homes, or trailers
- Churches, community organizations
- Offices, companies, and industries
- Retail stores, restaurants, shops, and markets
- Highways or busy streets with heavy auto traffic
- Side streets with sidewalks or bike paths
- Parks, playgrounds, and community centers
- Parking lots and garages
- Other things they may notice

Stage 3: Analysis

In this stage, the students should write a narrative of their exploration. The following questions might guide their writing:

- What did your observations tell you about the neighborhoods?
- How do people get from one place to another?
- Where do they gather to greet one another and talk?
- Is it a closely knit community? Are there distinctive ethnic groups?
- What cultures and peoples live there? How do you know?
- What else did you find?

Assessment

Students can be assessed on the clarity of their maps and drawings, the complexity of their ideas, and their ability to discuss what they have found.

ELEMENTARY MODIFICATION: DRAWING YOUR NEIGHBORHOOD

This is a modification of Project Idea 8.2 for younger students that can involve their parents as participants. Simply follow these procedures:

1. Convene students and parents in the classroom together. Any grouping is acceptable, although it may be good not to have children together with their parents to avoid undue influence.

2. Provide large sheets of paper and markers, pens, and other drawing tools

3. Ask the participants to draw their neighborhoods, as they know them. Ask them to focus on showing what is important to them and what they know really well. Give them enough time to explore their materials and think about what their neighborhood really means to them.

4. After everyone has had adequate time to complete their drawings, ask for volunteers (parents with their children) to share their work. Compare the results of parent and child. Quite often, each will present a very different-looking place. Have a discussion about how they differ. What did each person emphasize as important?

PROJECT IDEA: FAMILY ARCHAEOLOGY

From a general understanding of a neighborhood and its people, it is easy to move into family history. All people carry with them objects that are culturally meaningful. Such objects might include books, photographs, CDs, or a piece of clothing that was worn to a significant event. You can tap the power of objects and artifacts through this relatively simple classroom exercise, which you can build into a more extended lesson.

Start by talking to the students about the importance of objects and artifacts in people's lives. To stimulate their thinking, you might bring in some objects that are meaningful to you and talk about them. You can follow up with the assignment worksheet shown in Tool 8.3.

You can conclude the exercise with the classroom discussions or expand it to include writing about the object.

PROJECT IDEA: PLACE-BASED EDUCATION

Communities don't just happen. In any community, the people who live there have come to it for reasons, often many and complex. These reasons might be economic, such as the availability of jobs and work opportunities; cultural, such as the presence of other persons of the same ethnic group; or a particular quality of life or aesthetic, such as favorable climate, outdoor recreation, or scenery. Persons also live in places because they were born there and are connected to family and community.

Tool 8.3 Family Archaeology

Directions to Student

Talk with your parents, other family members, or other adults in your home. Identify one or more objects in your home that are important to your family's history. Such an object is called an *artifact*.

Find out more about the artifact. Why did your family keep it? Where did it come from?

Why is it important? How has it been used? A use might be *functional* in the everyday sense or it might have cultural, spiritual (i.e., religious), or social significance.

If possible, bring the object to class or bring a photo of it. Prepare a brief talk about the object and why it is important to your family.

What do we know about others in our community? Sometimes the answer can be surprising, as the following anecdote from Arizona demonstrates.

Filling in the Blanks

A pair of folklorists was conducting a residency in a small town in the White Mountains of the northern part of Arizona, a town with a population historically divided between Latter-Day Saints (Mormons) and Latinos. The two ethnic groups had largely lived separately for most of the twentieth century. The result had been that the schools tended to include Mormon parents but exclude Latino parents. "The Anglos were the newcomers to the area," a woman familiar with the town said. "It was the Latinos who started the town. They didn't think we wanted to include them. They'd been left out so often that they had given up on being included." She recounted the following story:

> Last year we had a historian come to the school to give a presentation on the history of the first Catholic priest in the community. Since it was a bleak stage behind her, we decided to roll down a backdrop that happened to be there. It had been painted for a Mormon celebration. It was of the town fifty years ago.
>
> As we sat there listening to the speaker, we could see that on the one side of town, the painting was very precise and detailed, with all the buildings clearly depicted. But as your eye drifted over to the other section of town, the Spanish neighborhood, the details got vaguer. And the buildings got smaller. Perspective was dropping off into a blur.
>
> And this woman sitting by me, a young Latina, turned to me and started pointing things out: "Did you know that the old saloon was right here, and this building was there, and . . ." I replied, "Barbara, I hate to tell you this, but I've never seen any old pictures depicting the Hispanic history of this town." The next day she called down to the diocese in Tucson, and they brought up pictures showing the other side of town clearly. So before the festival the next day, a bunch of us stood up on the top of a shaky ladder late at night, painting in the Hispanic part of town, putting crosses on the Catholic Church, finally giving validity to the other residents of the town.

This story is important because it shows that exclusion is often not a conscious choice but more a matter of habit or a lack of good information. Once the Anglo residents knew that they could help fill in the blanks in how they understood their own community's history, they began healing the rift that had divided the two cultures for generations.

Connecting a place to the identities of those who live there can be a powerful impetus to learning. It can directly achieve content standards in social studies and science while also addressing standards in English language arts and other subjects. It can stimulate higher-order thinking skills. Place-based lessons can revolve around such questions as

- What natural features contributed to the growth of our local economy?
- How did the growth of this economy impel our ancestors to move here?
- What factors have kept us here?

Understanding why your ancestors came to a particular place can be important, in that it can help you to better understand who you are. It can instill pride in your own family history and appreciation of the history of others. It is all about commonality and difference and how we can benefit through the appreciation of both. Project Idea 8.3 supplies a general framework for projects with this focus.

From the preceding relatively simple exercises and lessons, we turn to a project which involves in-depth exploration of family traditions, skills, and knowledge.

PROJECT IDEA: ENGAGING PARENTS THROUGH THEIR OWN TRADITIONS

Sometimes parents, especially those whose cultures have a strong tradition of respect for authority, believe that the teacher is the "expert" and thus they may avoid visiting the classroom or asking direct questions of the teacher. For teachers who are determined to make parents active partners, this tendency may prove a formidable roadblock.

But if a traditional art or craft is practiced in the home, this art form can be tapped for either a classroom lesson or a schoolwide festival, with the family member as a resident artist. Not only can this have the effect of appropriately honoring the parent, but it can also provide a powerful demonstration that the family's tradition constitutes a legitimate knowledge system that has been passed down over generations and that it encompasses unique, teachable information and skills. Through this, the parent may be elevated to a status equal to the teacher.

One exploding area of family artistry is the fantastic realm of fiber arts. For centuries, many families have worked in such media as sewing or embroidery, knitting or crocheting, lace making, or weaving. These traditions are deeply ingrained in many cultures, so much so that they may not even think of them as "arts" in the Western European and American sense of "fine art." Yet they belong in the same category. Many techniques have been handed down from mother to daughter over countless generations. Moreover, fiber arts are not just for girls: many fine tailors have been men, and boys have proved very adept at the fine motor skills involved in knitting—for example, in the Waldorf schools, where it is a common practice for children of both genders.

Cooking is an art, one that represents cultural diversity that you can smell and taste. Even within a tradition that is well known, such as Latino (or even mainstream Anglo), families pass down their favorite dishes over time. Many of these recipes represent unique experiences and life histories, which can be a source of engagement and learning, as well as innumerable interdisciplinary connections via recipes, to science (life sciences) and math (measurement).

Project Idea 8.3 **Place-Based Education**

Subjects

History/Social studies
English language arts

Grade Level

Various

Purpose or Rationale

Connecting a place to the identities of those who live there can be a powerful impetus to learning. It can directly achieve content standards in social studies and science while also addressing standards in English language arts and other subjects. It can stimulate higher-order thinking skills. Place-based lessons can revolve around such questions as

- What natural features contributed to the growth of our local economy?
- How did the growth of this economy impel our ancestors to move here?
- What factors have kept us here?

Understanding why your ancestors came to a particular place can be important, in that it can help you to better understand who you are. It can instill pride in your own family history and appreciation of the history of others. It is all about commonality and difference and how we can benefit through the appreciation of both.

Content Standards Addressed

- History/social studies, especially state and local history
- Various standards in English language arts related to research, writing, and presentation

Objectives

- Students will develop tools and methods for conducting historical research.
- Students will master techniques for writing and presenting their research findings.

Materials

Materials will vary depending on the project.

Grouping or Classroom Modification

A variety of classroom arrangements are possible, with additional field work outside of the school.

(Continued)

Project Idea 8.3 (Continued)

Parent or Family Role

Parents work as partners with students in the investigation of their communities.

Procedure

How to Begin

Use the following tools to plan and develop numerous lessons or units:

- Use the Four-Stage Planning Framework in Chapter 9 to begin thinking about a project.
- Start with Step 1 of the Framework. This involves either an artist's (or folklorist's) residency or writing and teaching a single lesson or brief unit.
- Develop a plan with the cooperation of parents and other teachers to move to the more advanced stages of the Planning Framework.

Use a tool like the Cultural Resources Inventory shown in Tool 8.4 to begin assembling a database of the kinds of resources in your community.

Collect Resources

There are many good resources on the Internet for planning a place-based component—a lesson, a unit, or an ongoing project. A good one to start with is the Rural School and Community Trust: http://www.ruraledu.org/topics/placebased.htm.

This site has numerous links, both internal and external, including a place-based learning rubric for assessing various aspects of a program, and a place-based portfolio system for collecting evidence of program effectiveness.

Assessment

Students can be assessed on their knowledge and understanding of local history, their application of research methodology, and their group work.

Tool 8.4   Cultural Resources Inventory

Directions to Student

Take this survey home and ask your parents, other family members, or other adults in your home to work on it with you.

Directions to Parents of Very Young Children

Read the questions to your child and take on the writing responsibilities, but still make it a joint effort with your child.

How long have members of your family lived in this state, community, or neighborhood?

How did the first family members that lived here arrive?

Where did they come from before that?

What interesting stories have been passed down from your parents or grandparents?

The preparation and sharing of foods can be a dynamic way to engage family members and provide a memorable time for students. You might showcase different cultural food offerings at a schoolwide potluck luncheon or via a more formal dinner prepared on campus for a Family Cultural Festival. And older students can even use food as a subject, compiling a cookbook of favorite recipes from their families.

Many traditions or skills reside in trades and professions, such as ceramics, carpentry, stone masonry, boat building, glasswork, printing, graphic arts, photography, industrial design, advertising, and so on. Many such things, occupational in nature, may push your own conceptual boundaries of what you consider to be art. This is fine. Art is an expanding universe.

Any family work, trade, or craft can become the anchor point for an entire lesson. For example, if one student has parents who farm, a parental presentation could become the focus for study of earth and life sciences, weather, and history/social studies—engaging parents, captivating students in meaningful inquiry, and meeting state content standards all at the same time. Project Idea 8.4 outlines the steps to take.

PROJECT IDEA: COMMUNITY DOCUMENTATION

Last we move to a project that integrates multiple subjects with the arts while tapping community engagement in varied ways.

A student documentary project can have the potential to engage students and parents in a comprehensive investigation of some aspect of the community. Such a project might focus on a local tradition or culture (e.g., ethnic artists or craftspersons), a problem or issue (such as pollution of a local waterway), or an interesting historic site (such as a local battlefield or historic home). Any subject is appropriate as long as it lends itself to visual or multimedia exploration.

The lesson plan in Project Idea 8.5 is designed to help students develop skills in community documentation using photography, video, and writing. It involves the definition and investigation of a topic or question related to the community, followed by extensive research in the field, and culminating with a public presentation.

This chapter has moved out of the disciplinary boundaries of the arts to explore the fabrics of communities. From here, it is a natural step to begin looking at some of the resources and partners that your community may offer and that you can use in your teaching. That search is the subject of the following chapter.

Project Idea 8.4 Engaging Parents Through Their Own Traditions

Subjects

Various

Grade Level

K–12

Purpose or Rationale

Parents will tap their own indigenous arts, crafts, and lifeways to become guest instructors in the classroom.

Content Standards Addressed

Various

Objectives

Students will understand and appreciate the varying contributions of members of the community.

Materials

To be determined

Grouping or Classroom Modification

To be determined

Parent or Family Role

Parents assume roles of visiting artist or demonstrators.

Procedure

How to Begin

- Talk about traditions in the class. Explain the concept and give some examples, perhaps brainstorming and generating a list.
- Involve the students in researching their families, using tools like the Home Skills Survey shown in Tool 8.5. Use the survey as a take-home exercise so that the children themselves explore the many traditions among their own family members and tradition bearers.

Planning

Compile the surveys and tally the results. Using such criteria as variety, diversity, connection to targeted standards, and potential for student (and parent) engagement, decide on a list of parental invitees. You may want to conduct a brief telephone or in-person interview with each parent on your short list to ascertain their readiness. While talking to them, make a list of any special materials or classroom modifications they may require. Then schedule each.

Students should be assigned active, rather than passive, roles—including small-group assignments to formulate appropriate questions to ask during and following the various demonstrations. They may also be required to write an essay or other verbal response or engage in a discussion following each parent's visit.

Assessment

Students may be assessed on their preliminary research with their family members, their questions and discussions, and final writing assignments.

Tool 8.5 Home Skills Survey

Directions

Take this sheet home. Work with a family member to complete it. Be prepared to talk about it during the next class meeting.

1. Is there some kind of work that a member of your family does that is a traditional art form or craft?

2. Describe what kind of work this is. How did the family member learn to do it?

3. Would the family member be willing to share what he or she does during a visit to the school? When might the family member be available?

Project Idea 8.5 | **Community Documentation**

Subjects

History/Social studies
English language arts
Media arts (visual art, photography,
   video, computer)

Grade Level

3–12

Purpose or Rationale

This lesson helps students develop skills in community documentation using photography, video, and writing. This lesson works best with a team approach: classroom teacher, media or tech specialist, volunteer or visiting artist or photographer or videographer, parents, and adult volunteers.

Content Standards Addressed

- History/social studies, including the study of local community characteristics and conditions
- English language arts, including the writing of scripts and narrative texts
- Media arts, including the selection and use of varied documentary media and the development of successive stages of a production

Objectives

Understandings

- Every local community has unique historical events, local conditions, problems, or issues that can be investigated through the documentation process.
- Some of these events or conditions can be researched through direct methods (documentation).
- Students can learn to use documentary methods to conduct their own research and present their findings.

Knowledge and Skills

- Identify a topic, issue, or question related to the community.
- Select appropriate documentary methods and media and use them to collect documentary evidence.
- Prepare and present documentation in the form of exhibitions or publications.

Materials

- Cameras (film or digital), video camcorders, or both
- Computers with digital imaging software and PowerPoint
- Film and videotape
- Large paper for storyboards, mat board, bookmaking supplies
- Sources: Center for Documentary Studies at Duke University: http://cds.aas.duke.edu

Grouping or Classroom Modification

Students will work in small teams with parent volunteers.

Parent or Family Role

Parents can be totally involved in a documentary project from the beginning. They may be tapped in the initial phase to work with their children during homework to identify ideas for a project. They can attend classroom meetings to help guide the discussion of what topics might be most useful to research. They can accompany the students as volunteers during the actual visual research. They may help significantly in bringing the final presentation to reality.

(Continued)

Project Idea 8.5 (Continued)

Procedure

Teaching the Lesson

Show the class slides of documentary photographs, including Farm Security Administration (FSA) photographers, such as Dorothea Lange, Russell Lee, and Walker Evans. Then brainstorm with the students, asking them, What do we see in these photos? The discussion should focus on

- The use of photography
- The depiction of significant topics or the investigation of questions
- The relationship between the medium and the messages

Talk to the class about the tradition of documentary photography and explain how it was used by the FSA in the Depression. The following questions can guide the discussion: Do you think that photography is still used for social documentation today? Are there other tools that we have today that could be used?

Divide the class into teams. Each team should brainstorm local history or current events. Following this initial group work, you should assign the students to talk with parents about ideas they might have. You may have the teams meet again to develop some ideas. Meet as a whole class and compile a list on an overhead or easel paper. Each team should then decide which topic they want to investigate from the list.

Next, conduct visual research. This is a relatively unstructured phase in which students collect still or moving images. Of course, your natural concern for student safety will guide the specific procedures that you suggest. The following are useful guidelines:

- Work with community organizations or local agencies.
- Work in teams with a responsible adult along on each visit to the field.

Hold the first group critique. Each team should put its preliminary work on display (e.g., in front of the class) and lead the class in a discussion of it.

- What is the topic being investigated?
- What ideas are emerging?
- What seems to be working?
- What next steps seem to be suggested?

Then continue with the following stages:

- Continued visual research, with periodic group critiques
- Development of narratives and text
- Decisions on presentation formats; possible options: a group exhibition, a book, a video, or a combination of several formats

The next stage is production. This may include the following:

- Printing and mounting of photographs
- Editing of video, including sound and narration
- Production of a PowerPoint slide show
- Design and installation of exhibition or design, layout, and publication of a book

In this final process, students might have the following roles: curators, docents, production designers, artists, exhibition designers.

Assessment

Students can be assessed on their journals and process notes and the final exhibition.

9

Tapping Community Resources

From the preceding chapter, it should be clear that families and communities possess incalculable riches. In this chapter, we consider some formal mechanisms for mining these riches to the betterment of student learning.

WORKING WITH COMMUNITY ORGANIZATIONS

If an informal assessment of your current resources indicates a need to supplement them, your school might benefit through collaboration with a community organization. You may already be familiar with the wealth of such entities that exists in your community. If not, you might begin by making a list of the following:

- *Museums.* Art museums can be especially important partners, particularly if a school lacks facilities and trained personnel to teach art. But you might also want to consider museums of history, ethnography, local culture, science, regional museums, or a children's museum, if your community is fortunate enough to have any of them.
- *Libraries.* Your community library is a very important potential partner, and not just in providing access to books. Today's libraries are incalculably valuable providers of all kinds of cultural materials and frequently serve as partners in school programs.
- *Other Organizations.* This category may include performing arts centers, visual art centers, and literary organizations. Such partners may help teach beyond their subject expertise.
- *Cultural Centers.* These are community organizations that celebrate the history of a specific people or ethnic group.

103

Photo 9.1   Student and adult mentor, Clark State Performing Arts Center, Ohio.
Photo by Beth Dixon.

Finding an Organization

How do you even begin to narrow down the possible choice of an organization? You might use any of the following strategies:

- Check your local telephone directory for a local arts agency (LAA) or a state association of LAAs.
- Log on to the Americans for the Arts database of members at http://ww2.americansforthearts.org/scriptcontent/index_members_search.cfm. You can search for a variety of types of organizations in your state or community, including LAAs.
- Contact your state arts or humanities council. They can provide a list of community organizations or artists in your community, as well as some good ideas for programs. Most state arts agencies have online databases or directories of artists and organizations that work with schools.
- The National Assembly of State Arts Agencies lists the state arts councils' Web sites and contact information: http://www.nasaa-arts.org/aoa/saaweb.shtml.
- The Federation of State Humanities Councils lists its member organization Web sites: http://www.statehumanities.com.
- Make a list of organizations or artists that seem promising.

Once you have made some preliminary contacts, you might begin by exploring some key ideas, either with your school colleagues (including parents) or with the organization that you've identified.

How might you work with such a potential community partner? Sometimes it makes sense to start on a small scale. The ultimate form of cooperation between a cultural organization and a school is an ongoing partnership. Such partnerships don't typically form overnight but grow over time. Tool 9.1, Types of School-Organization Collaborations, describes various types or stages of collaboration.

Tool 9.1   Types of School-Organization Collaborations

Model	Characteristics
Brief exposure	A performance, artist's visit, or unstructured field trip; no advance preparation or follow-through; curriculum connections absent
Extended exposure	Guest artist comes, an ensemble gives a performance, or students tour a museum or other community facility; some curriculum tie-ins, though not developed over time; performances accompanied by a teacher or student guide
Residency plus	Guest artists or others provide more than just instruction to students; may include short-term teacher workshop or provide resources that remain at the school; field trips fully supported by standards-based curricula guides
Systemic collaboration	More than just exposure; organization trains teachers, develops curricula; guest artists (scientists, historians) teach in classrooms
True partners	A formal arrangement between entities, sustained work over time; co-planning and co-development of curricula and lessons; teaching shared
Fused	School and organization essentially become a common entity; may occupy common space; co-teaching is the norm

Another way to look at the potential possibilities is through the planning framework found in Tool 9.2, which considers outside partnerships, as well as what happens in the classroom with curricula and teaching, and the degree of parent involvement. The tool describes four stages.

Assessing an Organization's Readiness

The most important criterion in selecting an organization is the presence in its mission statement of some service to children, youth, or schools. Before you enter an agreement, you want to ensure that the organization is ready for work with your school. Tool 9.3 provides a checklist for this process. Since the answers to some of these questions might not be obvious, some clues are provided.

Communicating With an Organization

Haley, a middle school teacher, is excited about using the local museum to help meet standards in social studies. Luis, the newly hired education curator at the museum, is equally eager to begin working with the school. But during

Tool 9.2   A Four-Stage Planning Framework

	Working With the Arts	Curriculum Connections	Parent Involvement
1	*Artists' Residencies.* An artist's residency can be a powerful stimulus to parental volunteer efforts. It is often the first step in an ongoing partnership.	*Single lesson* taught in one classroom on a one-time basis	*Marginal,* often involving only infrequent contacts, and then only as observers
2	*Partnerships.* Schools begin and deepen relationships with one or more community cultural organizations.	*Units and cooperative teaching,* which involve several teachers or learning over extended periods	*Frequent,* involving parental visits and participation in special events
3	*School Infrastructure.* This involves building dedicated spaces for exhibition, performance, and publication of student artworks that can instantly engage parents.	*Professional development and curricula integration* that weave the arts and culture seamlessly throughout the curriculum	*Extensive,* with continuous involvement both during and after school hours; includes participation in learning events as well as organizational and curricular leadership
4	*Sustainability.* Parent involvement and the arts are institutionalized within the school.		

Tool 9.3   Organizational Readiness Checklist

Criterion and Evidence	✓
The organization can provide needed resources in content areas, such as the arts, science, and history. *Clue:* Read its mission statement.	
The organization can help you to integrate curricula in order to meet standards of multiple content areas. *Clue:* Look at samples of previous work.	
The organization is geographically close.	
The organization can provide the school with additional needed technology or learning materials. *Clue:* Make a visit to its facility.	
Your school represents populations or community members whom the organization does not normally serve. *Clue:* Talk to organization staff about their visitorship.	
The organization represents a unique community resource.	
The organization's staff has expressed interest in working with your school. *Clue:* Talk to the staff.	
The students of your school are curious about working with a community organization.	

Photo 9.2   The Joe & Joan Martin Center, a unique learning partnership in Charlotte, North Carolina.

Photo by Valerie Rhymer.

their first meeting, they discover some communication problems. Haley mentions some things, like *content frameworks, Open Court,* and *pacing guides,* that Luis has never heard of. On the other hand, he uses several terms unfamiliar to Haley, including *ethnography, provenance,* and *docent.* They also stumble over some words both know, but have different meanings for, like *conservation* and *registration.* They frequently have to stop and check for mutual understanding.

Every field has its professional language or jargon, and often it doesn't translate readily into other fields. The cultures of schools and the cultures of nonprofit organizations are seldom the same. Yet constant and effective communication is essential to a school-community partnership (Sanders, 2006). Here follow some ideas about how to bridge differences that can make communication and joint planning challenging. And first, here are some of the ways that schools and their community partners differ:

Differences in Mission and Purpose

Public schools are charged with the PreK–12 education of children. They are held legally accountable to fulfill this mandate. Especially since NCLB, moreover, they face stiff sanctions if they do not meet specific benchmarks for improvement annually. Nonprofit organizations have no such requirement, but they still have missions that determine what kinds of programs and activities they can undertake. They are directed by independent boards, and if funded under certain programs, they must meet rigorous standards for demonstrating outcomes.

Differences in Training and Staff Knowledge

School personnel are steeped in the knowledge base of education, with specialized training for teachers, administrators, media specialists, counselors, and other personnel. Teachers must have knowledge of their content areas and professional practices, such as curriculum, classroom management, and assessment. Staffs of nonprofits often have diverse training, most often in a particular content area, such as art history or science. A relative few may be trained in museology or arts administration, which might include education courses.

Differences in Working Practices

Schools clearly approach teaching and learning in a variety of ways, but some attributes are common: the students are at the school all day; one or more teachers have primary responsibility for students on a continuous basis; and students work on extended lessons and problems, often using textbooks. Museums and other community educational institutions provide more temporary experiences, perhaps only during visits or tours.

Photo 9.3   Another view of The Joe & Joan Martin Center, a unique learning partnership in Charlotte, North Carolina.

Photo by Valerie Rhymer.

Finding a common language and a common set of working practices is thus a major challenge. Through exploring common purposes of community education and complementary needs and resources, you can forge a useful working relationship that bridges these divides of working culture.

Building Community Partnerships

Through their intricate community connections (board members, patrons, volunteers, visitors), community cultural organizations are ideal partners for schools in parent-involvement efforts. If you are fortunate enough to find such an organization interested in forming a partnership, you may be embarking on a journey which can transform your teaching and your school.

By their nature, partnerships are symbiotic relationships that afford mutual benefit. Organizations want to partner with schools because it helps fulfill their educational mandates (which many have) while building their audiences of the future. So it is a two-way street.

Partnerships have outside forces that impel them. For example, I have personally worked on, witnessed, or counseled community-school partnerships funded or supported by the U.S. Department of Education, the National Endowment for the Arts, the National Endowment for the Humanities, the National Science Foundation, the National Gallery of Art, and the Institute of Library and Museum Services. These are the federal tip of the iceberg; significant work is supported by state and local funds, as well. These various federal agencies' Web sites provide rich sources of information on grants programs in search of good ideas. The reason? Finding good outlets for their grants helps fulfill *their* missions to support effective educational programs.

Consider tapping some of these potential channels for synergy. A partnership may begin with a conversation and lead to a grant application on the way to remarkable, engaged learning for children.

10

Designing Spaces for Parent Involvement and Adult Education

In previous chapters we looked at a variety of arts-centered spaces and ways that you can develop these spaces, if you do not already have them. This chapter turns to two particularly important places in your school and considers how the arts can transform them. We begin where learning takes place and where the environment communicates everything to students.

DESIGNING THE ARTS-BASED CLASSROOM

When our niece Amy graduated from college with a master's degree in architecture, it was a time of great pride, and we naturally flew to Minneapolis to attend her thesis defense. During that visit, we toured her studio in the university's architecture department. Her own space, crowded against the cubicles and desks of many other young architects and designers of the near future, exhibited the controlled chaos of an inventive and busy mind: an economy of space was crammed with books, tools, drafts, models, works in progress, sketches, ideas, personal snapshots and other connections to life outside work, an alarm clock for quick catnaps during all-nighters, and maybe a half-finished snack that got interrupted by an inspirational flash.

It made me think that this is what a kindergarten class aspires to be—*aspires* but does not often attain. In the ideal space for young learners, there would be dedicated cubicles where students could work on their cherished ideas, keep half-finished work until it is done, and have all of the tools they need at their ready disposal.

Going up into the upper elementary grades, the reality falls even farther from this mark. Students sit in seats or at crammed desks and have to put their work away at fifty-five-minute intervals, as if they were shift workers in a widget plant. And beyond elementary, they even have to move from one room to the next at those same forced intervals. What happens in these rigid circumstances to the project left unfinished, the idea that just popped into a small head?

Elliott Eisner (2002) remarks that a school can feel like either a factory or a home. I suggest that it can also feel like Amy's architectural studio. The first choice is toward standardization, repetition, and conformity. The third is toward imagination, creativity, and diversity. I believe the first also harkens back to the schooling of Dickens's England while the third looks out into the future. This is a choice we have.

Although you do not have complete control over your classroom, especially over things like space and natural lighting, you have significant leeway to make it a creative place and move it toward the third model. You can start by asking some questions: What do I really want my students to be able to do? How can the space in which they work help this to happen? As your answers become clearer, you might be able to sketch out a new classroom layout that works better. As with many things in the real world, small steps may have to precede great leaps. You might need to look for resources, perhaps some of which can be donated by parents.

And this is where parent involvement can come into play. If you have parents who can dedicate the time, offer ideas, and perhaps assist in finding the resources, consider inviting a group of them to help design, plan, and reconstruct your classroom along creative lines. You may have to give up a little control, but you may reap incalculable creativity. And the Amys of the future, the ones coming into your room to learn, will thank you someday.

Although no consensus exists on what constitutes the ideal classroom for enhancing the arts and creativity, Tool 10.1 has a good initial list of desirable components, in checklist form.

DESIGNING AN ARTS-BASED FAMILY CENTER

A key to gaining the involvement of parents is having a place for them in the school. Such a place can provide a location for substantive work as well as a hub that anchors parents within the larger school culture. Parent centers have been pioneered successfully in many schools and have proved pivotal in giving parents a stake in their children's educational activities. A good example is the center at the James A. Foshay Learning Center in Los Angeles, California.

You can start a family center at a modest scale and grow it as needed. Initially, it might consist only of a small room, such as an unused office, with a part-time staff member on location or an office staff member looking in from time to time. Ultimately, it could turn into a fully staffed, full-time work environment, including afterschool programs.

Tool 10.1   Arts-Based Classroom Checklist

Criterion	✓
Colors on the floor, the rug, the walls	
Textures, with lots of variety	
Large geometric shapes, especially at early grades	
Print rich, with extensive examples of verbal literacy on walls	
Sound, music, aural stimuli	
Work centers for various intelligences	
Dedicated spaces or themed cubicles with realia (real-world objects)	
Multiple stations for writing	
Media, including CD, DVD, and iPods	
Computers with Internet connections, mass storage, and color printers	
Individual workstations or places to store projects in process	
Exhibition and gallery space for visual works	

The Role of Arts in a Family Center

A family center seems like an ideal place to display the power of the arts in student learning. This is especially true since it is apt to be the parents' first in-depth contact with your school and with the learning that takes place there, especially given the persuasiveness of the arts in communicating student achievement. In fact, you should not consider planning such a center without the arts as a central element.

The following section describes a process for building a center that is arts focused.

Finding and Designing a Space

Locate some kind of space that is potentially suitable, even if modifications will be needed. It should be close enough to the main office that parents can have easy access to it once they have signed in and so that clear directions and signage can easily direct them. The space should be large enough for comfortable chairs, tables and a desk for working, and display areas. The following steps should be next:

1. Designate a Design Team

This should involve parents as members. At the first meeting of the team, use the following questions to guide discussion:

- What will be the various functions of the Center? Will it be a place for parents to do learner-centered volunteer work at a remove from the classroom? What kinds of work might this entail? This discussion might reveal the following functions:
  - Providing a place to learn about the school for newly involved parents
  - Providing a neutral meeting place for teachers and parents where they can get to know each other and discuss substantive issues involving the students
  - Providing a space for gaining deeper understanding of standards and assessment
  - Providing a place to assist parents in becoming more helpful with homework and assignments
  - Housing adult education classes and seminars
  - Housing afterschool programs, such as the 21st-Century Community Learning Centers Program (further information on this program can be obtained from the U.S. Department of Education at http://www.ed.gov/programs/21stcclc/index.html)

- How can these functions be met? What physical arrangements of space, furniture, technology, and staffing will be necessary?

2. Develop the Space According to the Draft Plan

Use the worksheet shown in Tool 10.2. Have it reviewed by a variety of stakeholders, including administrators and staff, teachers, parents, and students.

This is an essential step. Your plan can benefit from the input of persons whose support will be critical to its success. Ask questions and use the answers to improve the plan. Use a survey similar to the Family Center Planning Survey found in Tool 10.3.

3. Infuse the Space With Student Art Work, Including Actual Examples of Visual Arts and Documentation of Performing Arts

A family center should be alive with student work. Such work can turn a center into a gallery, but with the work in it aligned with standards and providing actual evidence of student achievement. The student work can include visual arts, literature and writing, and videotapes or other documentation of student performances, presentations or projects.

The work should be carefully linked with important standards, with text explaining how the work provides evidence of standards being met.

4. Invite All the School's Parents to the Opening of the Center

Target a specific date for an open house. Develop a communications plan to announce the opening. Design and print a flyer or brochure and send it home via the children, requesting that they give them to parents or responsible adults. At the opening, have tour guides (students would be fine) to direct parents from the office to the center. Provide refreshments and other evidence of hospitality, and welcome visitors personally.

5. Staff It, Run It, and Constantly Monitor and Evaluate Its Progress

This is the last and critical step. Provide the continuous support that your family center needs and deserves.

This family center, as well as the other projects and lesson in the preceding chapters, should serve powerfully to bring parents into your school and involve them as volunteers, helpers, and often informal colearners.

PARENTS AS LEARNERS: ADULT EDUCATION IN THE ARTS

Now we turn to another role for parents, one that involves formal learning in the arts. One and a half centuries ago, John Ruskin had a vision of community centers where adults would gain education in arts and crafts. In a time when work was increasingly mechanized, dehumanized, and divorced from human craft, he saw this as an ennobling possibility, giving skills to factory workers that could arm them economically and uplift them morally. Ruskin is not widely read today, but his ideas are very resonant with many baby boomers, who display a voracious collective appetite for adult education. People want to keep learning, and this trend is likely to continue.

More than a century later, we can still tap Ruskin's ideas to create a powerful program in a school—one which serves as a magnet for attracting parents, family, and community members to learn alongside children and to gain valuable knowledge and skills in an art form.

Having such a program offers several advantages. It can help your school do the following:

- Maximize the use of dedicated school arts facilities
- Make the school a community center for evening and weekend learning
- Earn additional revenue for your school from registration fees
- Employ community artists as educators

Tool 10.2   Worksheet for Designing an Arts-Based Family Center

School: _____

Date: _____

Plan drafted by (planning team members):

Statement of need:

Functions of the center:

Description of center:
- Location:

- Additional construction needed:

- Materials needed and source:

Targeted completion date:

Tool 10.3   Family Center Planning Survey

School Name: _____ Date: _____

Dear Colleague,

Attached is the first draft of the proposed plan for a Family Center at our school. We value your input in helping this plan meet the school's needs. Please respond candidly and fully.

What are the most useful and feasible aspects of the draft plan?

_____

_____

_____

What parts of the plan may present challenges or difficulties in implementation?

_____

_____

_____

What kinds of challenges or difficulties do you foresee?

_____

_____

_____

How might the plan be modified to overcome these challenges?

_____

_____

_____

Please add any additional thoughts or comments:

_____

_____

_____

Respondent's Name: _____

Please return the survey in the attached addressed envelope. Thank you!

As with everything else, it is best to start small. You might use the following kind of multistage process:

- Include parents as learners in a visiting artist's residency.
- Provide a weekend workshop in the arts for parents.
- Provide space at the school for a local college or adult education center to teach arts classes.
- Develop an evening class for parents.
- Expand the evening class into multiple offerings during the day and evening hours.
- Develop scope and sequence (tying classes together so that they teach progressive skills).

Beyond the mastery of specific skills, adult programs can lead to much deeper insights. When talking about art, parents, teachers, and children can develop more sophisticated ideas about the meanings of artworks and cultural products in general: Why do we make art? Why do we write poetry, or perform, or sing? What is the role of art in our lives? These questions can lead to deeper understanding about the many, varied, and often profound roles of culture in everything that we do.

Developing a Schoolwide Parent Involvement Plan

If you have read the preceding chapters, you probably believe in the power of the arts to forge new, unique parent-school bonds. You have also had some practice, at least vicariously, in implementing some concrete ideas. Your next step is to put these ideas into a plan for your school. NCLB requires that every individual school or district must develop a comprehensive plan, possibly in partnership with a community organization but definitely with the involvement of parents. This chapter provides a step-by-step process for doing this. But you don't need to follow every step. Use what you need to begin, and fill the rest in later.

A good way to proceed is to get a three-ring binder. Copy some of the tools or lesson plans in the preceding chapters and use them as worksheets. When it is time to present your plan, you will have all the information you should need.

SURVEYING THE LANDSCAPE

Before you can implement steps to bring about more parent and family engagement, you need to assess the current status of parent involvement in your school. Then you can begin to formulate a plan based on that current picture. As you endeavor to learn more, you cast yourself in the role of the researcher, engaging other staff, parents, and even students in a process of gathering data to piece together a portrait of the current bridge that connects your school to its communities.

You may find during this process that your inquiry influences the results. Often the mere act of collecting information brings about desired aims. In education, one name for this is the *Pygmalion effect,* the concept that what we observe, we impact.

Sometimes these effects can be serendipitous, as another researcher and I found during our work with the Smithsonian Institution. We were conducting an evaluation of the Smithsonian's Museum Magnet School partnership with two schools in the Capitol Hill Area of Washington. One evening we convened a focus group of parents whose children attended the schools, in order to gain their perceptions of the program. As the focus group proceeded, we found that many of the parents knew less about the program than we had expected, and so the questions ended up flowing both ways. The interchange was lively and informative. After about one hour, we concluded the session, thanked the parents, and prepared to leave.

We were surprised that, rather than dispersing into the warm evening, the parents hung around in small groups and chatted about the program. Many of them were surprised at what they had learned. They engaged us in some of the conversations, which lasted for another hour. They talked about their own hopes for their children and their experiences with the sometimes troubled District of Columbia school system. Within a week, we were even more surprised to learn that these informal conversations had turned into a working group, a committee of parents committed to helping the program by volunteering and advocating for it. This group remained active through at least the duration of the project. A simple attempt on our part to collect data had incidentally turned into a supportive movement for education.

While these unanticipated effects can be welcome, your primary focus at this point is learning where your school is in the parent-involvement picture. I suggest you use a variety of sources of data, including informal interviews, focus groups, or observations.

PARENT INVOLVEMENT: WHAT DOES IT LOOK LIKE?

Schools are clearly not all alike, and parental or family involvement is not the same from one school to the next, either. In fact, one of the most important differences between schools may be the extent to which parents are involved and how that engagement manifests itself in the day-to-day activities of the school. Tool 11.1, the Parent Involvement Gauge, will help you assess your school's current level of parent participation.

Regrettably, there are many schools that fall into Phase 1. For them, much work remains. It is likely that most schools are in Phases 2 and 3 in this scale, with an exceptional few in Phase 4. The first step in any improvement plan is to help such schools gradually move into the next phase. Phase 5 is a vision to which all schools and districts should aspire. It is not impossible. This book is designed to provide tools for navigating that gradual journey.

Tool 11.1   Parent Involvement Gauge

Level	Characteristics
1	Parents largely stay away from the school except when a problem arises. Any communication is from the school to the parents.
2	Some parents visit the school during special events, such as Parents' Night and parent-teacher organization meetings; a few may be involved in volunteer efforts.
3	Some parents are involved in day-to-day activities. They visit the classrooms and observe lessons. They volunteer extensively in field trips and other events.
4	Most parents are involved. They visit the classrooms on a frequent basis and help out with lessons. They actively serve on the parent-teacher organization and meet frequently with school staff in shared governance. Parents and other adults may be learners in adult education programs.
5	The school and the community have become a common entity. Parents and other adults collaborate extensively with school staff, co-teaching and sharing the leadership of the school. The school is an intellectual hub of the community, with lifelong education taking place on a continuous basis.

ASSESSING SPECIFIC INDICATORS

In order to identify the most pressing needs in involving parents, it is necessary to determine several specific indicators (i.e., observable phenomena that demonstrate parent involvement). The first of these is parental presence in classrooms. The checklist found in Tool 11.2 is offered to help teachers assess this quality in their own classes.

Another important indicator is the extent to which parents support instruction through helping with homework and other forms of participation outside of the classroom—serving as *learning partners* with the teacher. This can be assessed using the checklist in Tool 11.3.

A third dimension (and checklist) is the extent to which parents actively advocate for school programs, especially in the arts. Assess it by using Tool 11.4.

Now how does your school stack up? If it is typical, there's room for improvement. This is where collaboration with a community cultural organization can come in.

WORKING WITH ORGANIZATIONS: ASSESSING YOUR SCHOOL'S READINESS

It is important at this point to assess another dimension: school readiness to work with a community organization. (In a previous section, we looked at a tool

Tool 11.2 Checklist: Parents in the Classroom

Criterion	✓
Parents provide contact information so that they can be easily reached.	
Parents usually come to special school events, such as Back to School Night.	
Parents visit the classroom to observe instruction and student work.	
Parents respond to communications from their children's teachers.	
Parents volunteer to help out at special events.	
Parents volunteer to help in the classroom.	

Tool 11.3 Checklist: Parents as Learning Partners

Criterion	✓
Parents ask questions about their children's assignments.	
Parents participate in their children's take-home assignments where appropriate.	
Parents request additional resources to help their children, when needed.	
Parents communicate with the teacher to clarify assessment and report cards.	
Parents help identify community resources that the teacher or their children can draw upon.	
Parents actively participate in parent-teacher organization meetings.	
Parents volunteer for assignments to committees.	

Tool 11.4   Checklist: Parents as Activists

Criterion	✓
Parents actively solicit funds from charitable organizations to help the school.	
Parents serve on the boards of, or volunteer to work for, nonprofits that work with the school as partners (e.g., the local art museum, Boys' and Girls' Club).	
Parents communicate with policymakers on behalf of the school.	
Parents write letters to the press providing support for the school.	

for assessing the organization's readiness.) The checklist in Tool 11.5 may help in this process and can help craft a powerful needs statement to help make the case to other teachers and administrators.

If you were able to check more than two or three of these, then there is probably significant potential for a school/organization collaboration.

PLANNING THE PROJECT

Once you've conducted a beginning needs assessment or survey of the current status, it's time to begin planning the project. This is where a meeting of all partners—including parents—is vital to get the ball rolling. Set a date, establish a meeting space and time, develop a list of possible attendees, and send out an invitation. In addition to staff and parents, the meeting should involve administrators. As with so much else in schools, the role of the principal is pivotal to the success of parent involvement efforts (Sanders, 2006). Early on in your thinking, invite the principal to be a part of the planning process and to the extent possible, the planning team.

Provide food and drinks, if possible. It's a great way to signal that guests are welcome and valued partners. But be considerate of special needs, such as vegetarian and religious food preferences, and always try to model healthy nutritional practices (Kyle, McIntyre, Miller, & Moore, 2006).

Tool 11.5   Checklist for Schools: Readiness to Work With a Community Organization (CO)

Criterion	✓
Your school perceives the need to emphasize content such as the arts and history for which teachers need additional preparation or resources.	
Your school is a magnet specializing in a content area represented by a CO.	
Your school perceives the need to integrate curricula in order to meet standards of multiple content areas.	
Your school is situated in geographic proximity to a CO that has educational capacity.	
Inadequate curricula resources (frameworks, lessons, etc.) limit your school's abilities in some content areas.	
Working with a CO offers an opportunity to seek and possibly secure additional funding.	
A CO may provide additional needed technology or learning materials.	
Working with a CO may help in involving parents and community members (e.g., working with the local Hispanic Cultural Center).	
Your community has unique resources (e.g., a large number of artists, a community museum).	
The staff of your school is curious about working with a community organization.	
The students of your school are curious about working with a community organization.	

Use the Planning Meeting Checklist and Agenda in Tool 11.6 to plan and conduct your meeting.

Working groups and responsibilities might include developing a gallery, a performing arts space, a literary journal, and so on.

In building effective partnerships, a team approach can be essential to success (Sanders, 2006). In turn, the early steps of planning, the convening of an effective introductory meeting, and careful and diligent follow-up with participants are essential to forging a team that will help ensure the implementation of your program.

Once you have a meeting, it is time to begin putting your plan on paper. Tool 11.7 provides a form to use. A filled-in example follows the blank one.

Sources for Ideas

The impetus for an arts project may come from a teacher, a community organization or a parent. It is vital to a true partnership to provide open channels of communication. Tool 11.8 shows an example of a survey to engage parents.

DEVELOPING INTEGRATED CURRICULA

As mentioned earlier, integrated lessons or units provide powerful tools for parent engagement. The template shown in Tool 11.9 provides a format for constructing such lessons. It will be familiar to readers of Chapters 3 through 8. In each cell of the table, fill in the information as indicated. If you need more space, you may photocopy either page, or type your own form. (Tool 11.9 is a blank template; Tool 11.10 provides an explanatory sample.)

FINDING FUNDING FOR YOUR PROGRAM

While many of the lessons and projects in *Building Parent Involvement* can take place with minimal funds, at some point you may want to investigate the potential for securing additional support to help your program grow. A brief summary of sources and strategies follows. Some of the sources will lead you to the more detailed information that is beyond the scope of this book.

Start Locally

If you are fortunate enough to have one or more foundations or public charities in your community, you may find that these organizations are willing to make grants to local schools or districts. Often, such entities maintain an emphasis on supporting local needs. A telephone inquiry or visit to the organization's Web site may give you this information. Such funders can be particularly attractive, since they may not require a complex or formal grant application. The Foundation Center (http://fdncenter.org/) maintains a database of foundations, searchable by community (a small fee is involved). But

(Text continues on page 132)

Tool 11.6 Planning Meeting Checklist and Agenda

Meeting Date: _____	Time: _____

Checklist of Materials

- ☐ Paper, pens, easels, markers
- ☐ Video, media, A/V (if needed)
- ☐ Project Planning Worksheet, one copy per participant (see Tool 11.7)
- ☐ Information (brochures, literature) on partners

Agenda

- Introductions
- Discussion of overall purpose
- Suggested working procedure, establishing working groups, defining tasks (a suggested list follows)
- Assignment to working groups and division of work
- Scheduling of future meetings of committee and working groups
- Assignment for "homework" for next session
- Open discussion of issues and ideas
- Adjournment

Tool 11.7 Project Planning Worksheet Template

School name:

Describe the project:

Which local resources will be used in the project?

How will they be used?

Identify the parents who will be involved:

Describe the parents' roles:

(Continued)

Tool 11.7 (Continued) Sample Project Planning Worksheet

School name:

Pine View Elementary, Pine View, Arizona

Describe the project:

Development of an interdisciplinary unit for Grades 2 and 3, combining science, art, and local history

Which local resources will be used in the project?

The Colorado Plateau Museum of Flagstaff

How will they be used?

Teachers will incorporate the Museum's learning guide, The Colorado River, for curricula and lessons.

Each class will make one visit to the Museum and tour its interactive learning center.

Identify the parents who will be involved:

Ms. Adams, Mr. Cruz, Ms. Dobson, Ms. Freire, Mr. Tenaya

Describe the parents' roles:

Parents will accompany students on museum tour, help with distribution of Discovery Boxes, work with students in making a Colorado River diorama, and serve as technical staff for an outdoor pageant.

Tool 11.8 Parent-Family Arts-Culture Project Survey

School Name: _____ Date: _____

Dear Parent: Thank you for your input. Please use this survey to identify and describe any ideas you have for a project that involves the arts, culture, or community history.

_____

_____

_____

What kinds of things might your child be interested in?

_____

_____

_____

What kinds of projects would you be interested in participating in? How?

_____

_____

_____

Respondent's Name: _____

Please return the survey in the attached addressed envelope. Thank you!

Tool 11.9   Integrated Curriculum Planning Guide: Template

School: _____

Name: _____

Subjects   **Grade Level**

Purpose or Rationale

Content Standards Addressed

Objectives

Materials   **Grouping or Classroom Modification**

Parent or Family Role

Procedure

Assessment

Tool 11.10   Integrated Curriculum Planning Guide: Explanatory Sample

School: Enter the name of your school here.

Name: Enter the names of persons completing the lesson or unit.

Subjects

List the primary and related content areas addressed in the lesson.

Grade Level

Identify the grade levels addressed in the lesson.

Purpose or Rationale

Provide an overall statement describing the purpose of or need for the lesson, based on knowledge of learners.

Content Standards Addressed

List the national, state, or district standards met by the lesson.

Objectives

List the knowledge and skills that students will gain from the lesson.

Materials

List any resources, equipment, materials, or supplies needed for the lesson.

Grouping or Classroom Modification

Describe any grouping of students or special arrangements to the classroom necessitated by the lesson.

Parent or Family Role

Describe how the project or lesson will involve and engage parents and family members. What roles will they have? How will their participation be solicited?

Procedure

Provide a detailed description of what happens during the lesson, including what the teacher and other educators do to begin the lesson and what students do as part of their learning.

Assessment

Describe procedures for assessing student learning, including authentic performances or tasks that students will generate, and tools (such as rating scales or rubrics) to be used for judging student work. Describe how you will evaluate the success of the unit, including meeting instructional goals, parent involvement, and overall effectiveness.

(Continued from page 125)

your librarian or district grants officer may also be able to help locate local givers.

A potentially huge source of support for school arts programs consists of noncash donations, often called *in kind* contributions. These may consist of such things as free printing and binding, the loan of technology or equipment, or the contribution of refreshments for a reception. Many local companies find that entering a partnership with a school is good for their public personae and consequently for their business.

State Funding Sources

While much state education funding is formula driven, funding in the arts tends to be more flexible. Every one of the fifty-six states, territories, and special jurisdictions (e.g., District of Columbia) has a public agency dedicated to the arts. Nearly all of these arts councils or arts commissions have an arts education grant program, and schools or nonprofit organizations partnering with schools are eligible applicants. Most of the arts education grants programs are aligned with the state's content standards. To find out what is available, go to your state arts agency's Web site and look for information on arts education or grants. To locate your state agency, go to the National Assembly of State Arts Agencies: http://www.nasaa-arts.org/aoa/saaweb.shtml.

National Funding Sources

While some arts funding is available at the national level, it is typically reserved for block grants to states or earmarked for organizations such as the Kennedy Center. The National Endowment dollars that go to state arts agencies are essentially pass-through funds, most of which are intended to be regranted by the states. Periodically, however, the U.S. Department of Education (USED) will announce a major arts education category for which schools and local education agencies are eligible. A watchful eye on the USED Web site or the Federal Register can often anticipate these. Again, many districts have persons who are specifically charged with the responsibility of watching for these opportunities.

Tapping Parent Involvement Funding From NCLB

With the passage by Congress of NCLB (2002), the nation entered a new era in parent involvement. For the first time, federal legislation not only set tangible outcomes for schools in terms of working with parents; it also provided for dedicated funding for meeting these outcomes and established sanctions for schools that do not meet them. The law requires, in part, that

A local educational agency may receive funds under this part only if such agency implements programs, activities, and procedures for the involvement of parents in programs assisted under this part consistent with this section. Such programs, activities, and procedures shall be planned and implemented with meaningful consultation with parents of participating children. (Sec. C)

This federal legislation has trickled down to state mandates, which are reflected in ongoing bureaus or offices of state education agencies. For example, California has a comprehensive plan for involving parents. In Ohio, the Department of Education has a dedicated Center for Students, Families and Communities. In Idaho, there's the Public School Parent's Network. The Washington State Office of Public Instruction has a dedicated Public School Parent's Network. Other states have similar programs designed to meet requirements of the federal legislation.

These state funds in turn are distributed to participating districts and schools, with the expectation that they will become part of a coordinated effort to engage parents and families in the education of their children and the daily life of the schools. Thus NCLB is both a carrot and a stick, providing opportunities as well as challenges. This is where the arts come in. One of the purposes of *Building Parent Involvement* is to help schools and districts to outline creative, arts-centered ways to tap funding from NCLB that is earmarked for this purpose. The following are ways to do this:

- In developing or updating your school's parent involvement plan under the requirements of NCLB, include one or more arts components. Describe how the arts program will help bring parents into the school community.
- If your district is an applicant or grantee under additional programs, such as Reading First or the 21st Century Community Learning Centers, you might find that an arts component is an ideal addition to the application or plan.
- Arts components of these plans should have specifically designated pockets of funding to ensure that the activities are fully sustainable.
- To coordinate the inclusion of your arts program in school or district plans, contact your district coordinator for NCLB, Title I, or other program, as appropriate.

Additional resources are available that can help steer your search. The Arts Education Partnership has published a useful guide for accessing federal funds for arts programs under NCLB. At the time of publication of *Building Parent Involvement*, the guide was available at http://www.aep-arts.org/PDF%20Files/NoSubjectLeftBehind.pdf. Also very useful is the National Network of Partnership Schools (n.d.) at http://www.csos.jhu.edu/P2000/. As with all Web site references, you may need to conduct a search if old links have expired.

This book is based on the vision of schools tapping the power of arts and culture, uniting communities and generations to ensure a better future. If you have read all the way to this point, then you probably share this vision. The next step is to actually implement plans that do all of these things. It may start with just a phone call to a parent, a casual remark, two minutes on the agenda at the next staff meeting, or some rough ideas written longhand over lunch. The main thing is to start and to keep building momentum to realize your vision.

12

Evaluating Your Arts Program

This chapter provides suggestions and tools to help you develop and implement a plan for monitoring your program and gauging its worth and value. Evaluating a program is important as a way to keep it on track; diagnose any problems that occur; improve it as you go along; ensure its success; and build support from the administration, the district, and the community.

But an additional reason compels you to evaluate. It is another way of involving parents in the school—as partners in the evaluation process itself. Now while many people readily accept the fact that a school should involve parents, they may find the notion that parents can be part of the evaluation of a program strange. Yet this is one of the most important places to involve parents. And this involvement, like so many other forms, should be *ongoing*—starting with the beginning—and *genuine*, representing an engagement at the deepest levels.

How do you do this? Start by asking parents to plan the evaluation with you. They should help frame the basic questions that guide all good evaluations. Such questions can be developed by a very simple process of asking parents: *What do you want to know?* The following are some types of questions that parents may want an evaluation to answer:

- What is the full range of arts programs being offered in the school?
- Are the arts programs increasing the amount and range of parent involvement in the school?
- Are the arts helping parents to understand what their children are working on?
- Are the arts bringing about more and higher-quality collaboration between parents and their children as learning partners?

135

- Are parents satisfied with the arts programs that are being offered?
- What additional arts offerings would parents like to have?

As you can see, some of the questions are descriptive, while others seek to determine the outcomes of programs. Each type of question is legitimate and useful.

These questions can be selected and agreed upon in a meeting of an evaluation subcommittee, a group convened for steering the evaluation process. This may be either a subset of your regular parent involvement group or a mixture of parents, some new to the program.

After deciding on guiding questions, the next step is to develop some instruments for collecting data. This is not as daunting as it sounds. These instruments may include an interview guide (basically a checklist of questions for conducting an interview or focus group) and a survey. Tools 12.1 and 12.2 provide an example of the former and a template for the latter.

USING ASSESSMENT FOR EVALUATION

Since the passage of NCLB, it seems that assessment is a large part of the daily routine in U.S. classrooms. But the high-stakes tests and the federal legislation behind them are all driven by a presumptive force: powerful interests—including policymakers and key voting groups—want to know how the schools are doing in preparing workers for the global economy and erasing achievement inequalities.

While the mismatch between these informational needs and the tools selected to meet them are at times lamentable, the situation nonetheless serves to illustrate one important principle: curiosity and the quest for information are capable of launching powerful movements. Put another way, if you ask questions, the universe will begin moving toward the answers.

So as an educator, the best way to take control of the assessment process and the uses (and misuses) to which assessments are put is to decide what *you* want to know. What questions do you have about student achievement? What can the assessments in your own lessons and units, along with information from high-stakes tests and other sources, tell you about students' mastery of challenging content and standards?

Throughout this book, the emphasis has been on authentic, performance-based assessment tasks. Such assessments can be as psychometrically rigorous as standardized tests while possessing the validity—the relationship to meaningful content—that the latter may lack.

DOCUMENTATION FOR EVALUATION

Documentation, meaning the use of photography and video to record activities, is a powerful source of data for an evaluation. It can answer the following kinds of questions: What learning activities are students engaging in, and how do

Tool 12.1 Interview Guide: Southside Elementary Parent Partners Program

Directions to Interviewer

Ask each question and follow-up questions as needed. Record interview or take careful notes.

Interviewer: _____

Interviewee: _____

Date: _____

1. How much do you know about the arts programs at the school?

2. How did you find out about the programs?

3. Are your children involved in any of them?

4. Have these programs been beneficial for you or your children? In what ways?

5. How might these programs be improved?

Tool 12.2 Survey Template

School _____ Project Name _____

Directions for Part 1

Please rate each statement on a scale of 1 through 5 by circling the appropriate number. Use 1 for *strongly disagree* and 5 for *strongly agree*.

Question 1	1	2	3	4	5
Question 2	1	2	3	4	5
Question 3	1	2	3	4	5
Question 4	1	2	3	4	5
Question 5	1	2	3	4	5
Question 6	1	2	3	4	5
Question 7	1	2	3	4	5

Directions for Part 2

Answer the following questions in the spaces provided. Use additional sheets if necessary.

Question 8

_____

_____

_____

_____

Question 9

_____

_____

_____

_____

Question 10

_____

_____

_____

_____

Thank you.

they evidence the mastery of challenging content? How extensive is parent involvement? What kinds of activities are parents becoming involved in?

It is really important to involve parents as documentarians. By putting them behind the camera, you charge them with looking for evidence of involvement, which can in turn increase their own involvement. Some parents might hesitate to take on such a role because of their own perceived lack of technical skill. However, you can get their feet wet with a relatively simple assignment, such as taking pictures with a point-and-shoot camera. As they become more comfortable with this role, they might take on the more challenging assignment of capturing a lesson with a camcorder.

Digital media can capture a range of evidence of student learning, including artwork, performances, and multimedia portfolios.

DEALING WITH DATA

The amount of data that ensues from an evaluation can quickly outrun your ability to keep track of it, if you don't develop a system. In fact, it is important that you can store your data *and* that you can access it when you need it—whether for a parent conference, a report to the school district, or an advocacy piece to be prepared for a local television station. Control of information is a powerful prerogative you will not want to relinquish.

Develop a filing system for storing and retrieving data, including interviews, surveys, and documentation. While a conventional paper filing system may be adequate for much of the information, if you are using digital media, you might also investigate the use of CD-ROM and DVD as exciting ways to capture, store, organize, and retrieve large amounts of data.

The image-rich, multisensory future into which education is moving is strongly propelled, as previous generations' futures have been, by the artistic tools of hands and minds. It is a journey which no thoughtful teacher, student, or parent would want to miss.

Bibliography

Anderson, T. (1993). Defining and structuring art criticism for education. *Studies in Art Education, 34*(4), 199–208.

Bloom, H. (1998). *Shakespeare: The invention of the human.* New York: Riverhead.

Boult, B. (2006). *176 ways to involve parents* (2nd ed.). Thousand Oaks, CA: Corwin Press.

Bransford, J. D., Brown, A. L., & Cocking, R. R. (2000). *How people learn: Brain, mind, experience, and school.* Washington, DC: National Research Council.

Burton, J. M., Horowitz, R., & Abeles, H. (2000). Learning in and through the arts: The question of transfer. *Studies in Art Education, 41*(3), 228–257.

C.A.R.T.S. (Cultural Arts Resources for Teachers and Students) Available at http://www .carts.org/.

Catterall, J. (2002). The arts and the transfer of learning. In R. J. Deasy (Ed.), *Critical links: Learning in the arts and student academic and social development.* The Arts Education Partnership. Available at http://www.aep-arts.org/PDF%20Files/ CriticalLinks.pdf.

Center for Arts Education. *Involving parents and schools in arts education: Are we there yet?* Available at http://www.cae-nyc.org.

Center for Comprehensive School Reform and Improvement. *Meeting the challenge: Getting parents involved in schools.* Available at http://www.centerforcsri.org.

Chadwick, K. G. (2004). *Improving schools through community engagement.* Thousand Oaks, CA: Corwin Press.

Creating a Family Center. Wisconsin Department of Public Instruction. Retrieved March 1, 2005, from http://www.dpi.state.wi.us.

Davis, M. R. (2004, May 12). Guidance on parental involvement issued. *Education Week* Available at http://www.edweek.org/.

Deasy, R. J. (Ed.). (2002). *Critical links: Learning in the arts and student academic and social development.* The Arts Education Partnership. Available at http://www.aep-arts .org/PDF%20Files/CriticalLinks.pdf.

Delgado-Gaitan, C. (2004). *Involving Latino families in schools: Raising student achievement through home-school partnerships.* Thousand Oaks, CA: Corwin Press.

Eisner, E. W. (2002). What can education learn from the arts about the practice of education? *The encyclopedia of informal education.* Retrieved May 22, 2005, from http://www.infed.org/biblio/eisner_arts_and_the_practice_of_education.htm.

Epstein, J., Sanders, M., Simon, B., Salinas, K., Jansorn, N., & Van Voorhis, F. (2002). *School, family, and community partnerships* (2nd ed.). Thousand Oaks, CA: Corwin Press.

Fiske, E. (Ed.). (n.d.). *Champions of change: The impact of arts on learning.* Washington, DC: Arts Education Partnership and the President's Committee on the Arts and the Humanities. Retrieved May 25, 2005, from Arts Education Partnership Web site: http://aep-arts.org/PDF%20Files/ChampsReport.pdf.

Gardner, H. (1983). *Frames of mind: The theory of multiple intelligences.* New York: Basic Books.

Goleman, D. (1995). *Emotional intelligence.* New York: Bantam.

Hughes, J., & Wilson, K. (2004). Playing a part: The impact of youth theatre on young people's personal and social development. *Research in Drama Education, 9*(1), 57–72.

Idaho Commission on the Arts. (2005). *Final Grant Report, Northwest Children's Home.* Boise, ID: Author.

Jensen, E. (2001). *Arts with the brain in mind.* Alexandria, VA: Association for Supervision and Curriculum Development.

Kendall, J. S., & Marzano, R. J. (2004). *Content knowledge: A compendium of standards and benchmarks for K–12 education.* Aurora, CO: Mid-continent Research for Education and Learning.

Kyle, D., McIntyre, E., Miller, K., & Moore, G. (2002). *Reaching out: A K–8 resource for connecting families and schools.* Thousand Oaks, CA: Corwin Press.

Kyle, D., McIntyre, E., Miller, K., & Moore, G. (2006). *Bridging school and home through family nights.* Thousand Oaks, CA: Corwin Press.

MacLachlan, P. (1994). *Skylark (Sara, plain and tall).* New York: HarperCollins.

Merberry, J., & Bober, S. (2002). *A magical day with Matisse.* San Francisco: Chronicle Books.

National Center for Family and Community Connections With Schools. Available at http://www.sedl.org/connections/research-syntheses.html.

National Network of Partnership Schools. (n.d.). Available at http://www.csos.jhu.edu/P2000/.

No Child Left Behind Act of 2001, Pub. L. 107-110 (2002). Retrieved June 15, 2006, from www.ed.gov/nclb/.

North Central Educational Laboratory. (2006). *Literature review of school-family partnerships.* Available at http://www.ncrel.org.

O'Connor, J., & Hartland, J. (2002). *Henri Matisse—Drawing with scissors.* New York: Grosset & Dunlap.

Perkins. D. N., & Tishman, S. (2001). Dispositional aspects of intelligence. In S. Messick & J. M. Collis (Eds.), *Intelligence and personality: Bridging the gap in theory and measurement.* Maweh, NJ: Erlbaum.

Rauscher, F. H., Shaw, G. L., & Ky, K. N. (1993). Music and spatial task performance. *Nature, 365*(6447), 611.

Sanders, M. (2006). *Building school-community partnerships.* Thousand Oaks, CA: Corwin Press.

Shelley, S. L. (1999). *A practical guide to stage lighting.* Woburn, MA: Focal.

Sikes, M. (1992). *Evaluation of the Artist-in-Residence Program, Arizona Commission on the Arts.* Unpublished report.

Sikes, M. (2005a). Improving Washington's schools. An evaluation of the Community Consortium Grants Program, 2003-2004. Retrieved June 20, 2006, from http://www.arts.wa.gov/progAIE/pdf/consortial%20eval%20final%20report%2005.pdf.

Sikes, M. (2005b). *Literature review of arts education research.* Prepared for the Ohio Department of Education.

Urschel, J. (1994, March 15). Why Johnny can't dance. *USA Today,* p. A8.

Weiss, H. B., Faughnan, K., Caspe, M., Wolos, C., Lopez, M. E., & Kreider, H. (2005). *Taking a closer look: A guide to online resources on family involvement.* Harvard Family Research Project. Available at http://www.gse.harvard.edu/hfrp/projects/fine/resources/guide.

WestEd. (2004). *Evaluation of the California Arts Council's Arts in Education Demonstration Projects: Final report.* Available at http://cac.ca.gov/wested/westedfull.pdf.

Winner, E., & Hetland, L. (Eds.). (2000). The arts in education: Evaluating the evidence for a causal link. *Journal of Aesthetic Education, 34*(3–4), 3–10.

Index

CORWIN PRESS

The Corwin Press logo—a raven striding across an open book—represents the union of courage and learning. Corwin Press is committed to improving education for all learners by publishing books and other professional development resources for those serving the field of PreK–12 education. By providing practical, hands-on materials, Corwin Press continues to carry out the promise of its motto: **"Helping Educators Do Their Work Better."**